Nobody's Wife

Nobody's Wife

The Smart Aleck and the King of the Beats

Joan Kerouac

INTRODUCTION
by
Jan Kerouac

FORWARD
by
Ann Charters

CREATIVE ARTS BOOK COMPANY
Berkeley • California

Nobody's Wife is published by Donald S. Ellis
and distributed by Creative Arts Book Company

For information contact:
Creative Arts Book Company
833 Bancroft Way
Berkeley, California 94710
1-800-848-7789

Library of Congress Cataloging-in-Publication Data

Kerouac, Joan, d. 1990
    Nobody's wife / Joan Kerouac.
        p. cm.
    ISBN 0-88739-368-3 (alk. paper)
    1. Kerouac, Jack, 1922-1969--Marriage. 2. Kerouac, Joan, d.
1990--Marriage. 3. Authors, American--20th century--Biography. 4. Beat
generation--Biography. I. Title.
    PS3521.E735 Z738 2000
    813' .54--dc21

                                                    -                    00-060278

ISBN 0-88739-368-3

Printed in the United States of America

Introduction

Jan Kerouac

During the last ten years of my mother's life, her constant preoccupation, aside from the garden, was to write this book.

I remember watching her, her bony frame in her favorite antique turquoise sweatshirt, shuffling over to sit down at her typewriter. It was an ancient machine, covered with tobacco dust. She would sit down every evening, or whenever she got a chance, and between intermittent gulps of coffee, and drags on her hand-rolled Bugler-tobacco cigarettes, she would tap away with one finger on each hand.

She started writing the book in 1980, just after she was diagnosed with breast cancer. The doctors told her she had a year or so to live. But she was determined to hang on, to prove them wrong, to last until she could get the book on paper. She went through periods of remission and illness, had a double mastectomy, and still kept writing.

She could get going really fast with only her two index fingers, because she was telling her stories, the accounts of her young adulthood. Often I was there with her in her little wooden house in Eugene, Oregon, listening to the squealing brakes from the hump yard nearby. There was a family of possums living under

v

the house, and they'd be bumping around. My mother would come into the living room, where I was, and we'd talk and talk, and then we'd talk some more. She was my greatest friend and confidant.

I watched my mother, over and over again, trying to get the first sentence of the book right. She was such a perfectionist. In fact, I don't think she would have ever finished this book if she had lived, because she used to write the first sentence over and over again, and she was never satisfied with it. It's fortunate that she did spend some time writing all the other sentences.

She died in 1990. When it came time to clean out the worn little house, my brother David and I flipped a coin to see who would do the fridge and who would clean underneath the bed. I lost the toss and had to face that mountain of paper under the bed. I was sneezing and coughing because there was so much tobacco dust in among the papers. We knew the book wasn't finished, so I just put all the crumbling paper-clipped pieces into a box, and David put the box into his attic, and it stayed there for three years.

Then a very special fellow came along to put all those pages in order—David's brother-in-law, John Bowers. John read through the pieces my mother had written, became very excited about its potential, and asked David and my sisters and me for permission to organize it and weave it together and edit it for publication. He ended up working on it for almost two years, and I think he's done an exceptional job. He had to put everything together like a puzzle, all the fragments of chapters. I know my mother's voice so well, and John has done wonderful work, keeping that voice intact on every page.

Reading it reminds me of listening to her telling me her anecdotes. She was a great storyteller, as you'll see when you read this. I knew that any time of day or night, I could go up to her and say "Mommy? What happened on that night in 1950, when Jack yelled to you from the street and you threw down the key to your loft?" And she would clear her throat, take a gulp of coffee, and launch into the whole fascinating story. I really miss that.

In fact, one thing I realized a few years ago is that the stories of my childhood perished along with my mother. No one else knew me when I was a baby—just her. So with her died all the knowledge and all the memories of me as a baby. I'm sorry she didn't write all those years as part of her book. It's a hard thing for an adult child to come to terms with—that never again will you be able to ask someone what color dress you were wearing in Central Park that day in 1953, or whether you had tantrums, or whether you got along well with other children. I have to be content now with just having what I recall, and I miss being able to listen to her memories.

As my mother worked on this book, she had various titles in mind. One of them was *Smart Alecky Basketweaver*. In 1979, she briefly got back together with Herb Lashinsky, who had been her lover nearly thirty years before. The first time she first met my father Jack, she'd been with Herb in her loft, as you'll read here. Sometime in those intervening years, Herb sent her a card with an ugly cartoon picture of an Indian weaving a basket, and the caption said "One thing I can't stand is a smart-alecky basketweaver."

That was how Herb felt about her, that she was a primitive and didn't really know anything. She was a woman, she was uneducated. Yet she had ideas, these incongruous abstract scientific concepts. It infuriated Herb, who was a scientist, that she had no credentials but would still attack these weighty topics in genetics, philosophy, anything that attracted her attention.

My mother had hopes that she and Herb would finally be together after that reunion meeting, but within just a few months, Herb died unexpectedly. Then, right after that, she received the blow of her cancer diagnosis. She started writing then, and at first the whole book was supposed to be about her relationship with

Herb, but as she went on, she came to realize that the stories she really wanted to tell were about Jack Kerouac and Bill Cannastra and, Neal Cassady, too.

Herb, and sometimes Bill and Jack too, reminded her of her mother. Anybody who scoffed at her or told her she couldn't do something the way she wanted, reminded her of her mother. Maybe that was the key to her strongly independent personality that made her do so many rebellious things in her life. My mother spent most of the days of her life trying to prove to people that she could do anything she set her mind to.

One day, I was sitting in the front yard in Eugene, watching her pace back and forth along the street, carrying a shovel. A guy from down the block came walking by, and he looked at her, and said, "What are you doing?"

And she said, "I'm planting tomatoes." She started shoveling, right then and there, in the front driveway.

He gawked at her like she was crazy and said, "You can't plant tomatoes in the driveway!"

She stared right back at him and answered defiantly, "Oh, no? You'll see. Just watch me. I'm going to plant tomatoes here, and you'll be envying them all summer."

And he did. She added a whole pile of compost to the driveway and planted the tomatoes in that, and throughout the summer she tended those plants. They were succulent and delicious, and she made sure the neighbor guy knew it.

And now, as she looks down from wherever she is, she can see that her biggest project is finally finished. She struggled for ten years to tell her story, and at last that dream has come true. She's glad for it, I know, and she knows that it turned out really well.

And finally, she can say to the world, "See? Here it is. I told you I'd do it."

Foreward

Ann Charters

On February 20, 1962, Jack Kerouac reluctantly met his second wife Joan Haverty after years of being divorced. She was suing him for financial support of their ten-year-old daughter Janet, whom he had never seen. Joan had separated from their seven month marriage in 1951, after she became pregnant and Kerouac said he was unwilling to be a father, accusing Joan of infidelity. When they were together, she had worked as a waitress to support him while he was writing the manuscript that became *On the Road*.

At the time they went to court, Joan was supporting her other three small children as well as Janet. Meanwhile, Jack had become the famous author of the best-selling *On the Road*, which would be followed by *The Dharma Bums*, *The Subterraneans*, *Doctor Sax*, and *Maggie Cassidy*, as well as a book of experimental poetry and two prose sketches. He was also infamous after his invention of the term "Beat Generation," which he had defined as "a swinging group of new American men" who were "intent on joy" because they possessed "wild, selfbelieving individuality."

Against his will, Jack agreed to submit to a blood test, which proved inconclusive, despite his daughter's striking resemblance to him. At a hearing in a judge's chambers on March 12, 1962, which also was Kerouac's fortieth birthday, he agreed to pay fifty-two dollars a month for Janet's expenses. Jack wanted the record to show that he was not the father of the child, "only that she bears my name." At the end of the month, trying to put a positive spin on what he considered a bad deal, Kerouac bragged to his editor Robert Giroux that the judge had heard of his books and been impressed with him as an "exponent of a new philosophy."

Besides the small sum granted in a court of law for the support of a well-known writer's only biological offspring, there's a painful irony in Kerouac's last letter, composed seven years later. On the day before he died, Kerouac wrote to his young nephew Paul Blake in a futile effort to name him as the final beneficiary of his estate. Kerouac belatedly realized the colossal importance to him of what he called "someone directly connected with the last remaining drop of my direct blood line."

Janet was not mentioned in the letter, nor in Kerouac's will. She kept as the only souvenir of her meeting with her father the cork from the bottle of Harvey's Bristol Crème sherry that he bought in a Lower East Side liquor store and finished in the kitchen of Joan Haverty's tenement apartment in 1962, after submitting to the blood test. Later, Janet also had Jack's agreement, after she paid a surprise visit to his home in Lowell, Massachusetts in 1967, that she could call herself Jan Kerouac if she wrote a memoir about her life on the road. He told the rebellious fifteen-year-old, "Yeah, you go to Mexico and write a book. You can use my name." Jan's book, *Baby Driver*, was published in 1981. It carries an affectionate endorsement by Lawrence Ferlinghetti: "The reader will know Jan Kerouac to be the true daughter of old sweet Jack, on her own wide road."

Now, for the first time, Joan Haverty tells her side of the story in *Nobody's Wife*. She proves herself to be a remarkable chronicler of her era. We can prize her honesty in her poignant description of the perils of heart and spirit facing a bright, insightful female barely out of girlhood seeking an independent life in early 1950s' New York. Joan's memoir is more than a sensitive evocation of her difficult coming of age; it also fills an important gap in the Jack Kerouac story. For the first time, we can read a detailed account of Kerouac's life "off the road" with his widowed mother, Gabrielle, candidly recounting their dependence on each other.

I can verify the truth of Joan Haverty's observations. In 1966, fifteen years after she moved out of Kerouac's life, I was a visitor for two days in the household in Hyannis, Massachusetts, where Jack lived with his mother. While he helped me compile his bibliography, I saw Jack interact with Gabrielle and heard their conversations. Joan was a sharp and accurate observer. Jack and his mother come alive on these pages, along with Neal Cassady, Allen Ginsberg, Lucien Carr, Bill Cannastra, and other figures in the Kerouac legend. Joan knew some of them only briefly, but she captures their essences in this book. As Kerouac wrote Cassady in late 1950, before his marriage had begun to erode, he believed that Joan, too, was a writer. "She really knows how to write from instinct & innocence. Few woment can do this. Joan Kerouac...a new writer on this old horizon. I see me & her cutting around the world in tweeds, yass..."

Jack Kerouac died of hemorrhaging esophageal varices in 1969. Joan Haverty was taken by cancer in 1990. Jan Kerouac wrote a second book, *Trainsong*, and had been working on a third, *Parrot Fever*, when she succumbed to renal failure in 1996. Father and daughter continue to live in the imaginations of millions captivated by the literature they created. Now, Joan's fiercely individualistic spirit radiates in this, *her* literary legacy. Read on and see.

Fact is the mother of memory; viewpoint its wayward father.

— Anonymous

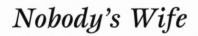

Nobody's Wife

Chapter One

I opened my eyes in darkness, and my mind was tangled between the haziness of a dream, the warmth of a memory, and the whisper of a voice from the future. I lay in my small bed, in my mother's house just outside Albany, working around the images and trying to separate the dream from the memory from the vision.

In the dream, I'd been looking over the sparkling lights of Manhattan. I sat on steel, high above the ground. There was a tart chill in the evening breeze.

Looking over the city, I heard a voice inside me. There was a voice in my womb, and it was a daughter, and she made me happy. But I couldn't hear what she was saying, so I gazed across the city, drifted over it, and then I landed on the ground and I was running. I was a child, hurrying home to tell my granddaddy about a discovery I'd made. I burst into the kitchen where my mother was fixing breakfast.

"Don't you bother your granddaddy," my mother said. "His back is hurting."

I went down the hall and stood by his open door.

"Is that you, Joanie?" he asked.

"Yes." I moved into his view and I could see him on the bed. "Does it hurt very badly?"

"Come in, honey. It's getting better, I think."

I sat on the carpet beside his bed and told him, "Granddaddy, I've found the most beautiful thing! And I can't bring it to you, and the sun will spoil it."

Then he and I were floating across an empty field to a row of low shrubs, where a spider had spun her web. It was perfect, spangled with dew drops catching the light like crystal beads.

"It's beautiful, honey," Granddaddy said. "I feel better just seeing it."

The warmth of his smile became the warmth of my bedding around me, but I wasn't willing to let him go. In my room, with the steady sound of a lonesome cricket outside, I followed the rest of the memory. I remembered how I'd looked at my granddaddy, and I knew his back still hurt. I loved him so much. Who else would ever make such an effort for me? Could I ever be that kind of a friend to somebody I loved?

"Granddaddy," I asked him, "how does the spider know how to do that?"

"What does your teacher have to say?" he replied.

"Instinct!" I made a face.

"You don't like that explanation?"

"It doesn't tell me where it came from. You know, how it got into the spider."

"How about God? Do you think God told her how to do it?"

I considered that. "That's more like it, but you know, Granddaddy, that God doesn't whisper into each spider's ear how to spin a web."

"Do spiders have ears?" he asked, and we both laughed at the picture.

"It had to begin with the first spider, Granddaddy, didn't it?" I prodded. "Everything about how to make a web was inside the first spider."

"Of course, honey, but once there were no spiders," he gently noted. "Where was all that knowledge then?"

The question took me by surprise. "Oh, Granddaddy," I almost whispered. "In the very first life?" I paused, turning this over in my mind, while my grandfather watched, smiling. "Was there always life?" I asked.

"That I don't know. But I know there was always something to know. There was always the information that sustains life."

I wanted to hug him but was afraid of hurting his back. "How do you know?" I asked him.

"I guess I learned it from the cactus and the spider and the tide."

We started back to the house. I was full of wonder, still amazed, examining this idea, seeing how it fit with everything I knew. "Just think!" I finally burst out. "If God gives a spider or a cactus so much, just think of all the knowledge he must have given us!"

Granddaddy had smiled, taking my hand in both of his, adding "And do you know what else God gave us?"

"What?"

"All the tools we need to learn the things we don't know."

I had been drifting back to sleep, but now I sat up in bed with a start, the feeling of my granddaddy's hands warm around mine after all these years, and an empty place waiting for a daughter tumbling inside my womb. And I had the intuition that I was about to learn more than I had ever expected to know about the world. It was a clear spring night in 1949, I was 19 years old, and I was eager to start.

Chapter Two

The dream was still clinging to me, just as the web had clung to the bush, late the next evening. Cliff Pryat and I were driving back to Albany from the Tanglewood Music Festival, and Cliff was going on and on about Mary Bea, a woman he knew in Provincetown.

"She runs a quiet place, a retreat, for serious artists. Painters and writers mostly. The type of people you want to meet," he said. He looked over at me, appraisingly. "I'll be going up there for two weeks this summer. How would you like to go with me?"

I thought it over, looking back at Cliff. "I'm going up to Provincetown anyway," I told him. "I thought I'd get a room where I stayed last year, but I suppose I could meet you at Mary Bea's instead. Would I have to reserve a room?"

Cliff smiled. "No. There'll be a room. No need to worry about that."

I assumed that if anyone would know about an artists' retreat, it would be Cliff. He was the music, art, and theater critic for Albany's *Knickerbocker News*. We'd met when I was a bit player at the Albany Playhouse, and it was lucky for me that we had. At seventeen, I was the youngest member of the troupe. The others were up from New York, street-wise and stage-wise too, and I was out of my depth. Cliff was a tall, thin, erudite gentleman of fifty-two, and he had taken on the role of my guide and protector. In this bewildering environment, I welcomed a man to be that for me. He was at every cast party, and before long he was taking me to the opening nights of ballet, opera, and theater productions within easy driving distance of Albany, as well as local art shows and cocktail parties. I looked at it all as a valuable experience, and I worked to develop poise and self-confidence, glad for the chance to meet interesting and stimulating people. I considered myself fortunate to have Cliff for a friend and teacher, realizing that had I been dating men close to my age, my experience might have been stock car races and drive-in movies.

I thought Cliff enjoyed the role of teacher and was entertained by my companionship. Was there another motive behind his squiring me around? I was unaware of it. He felt I had a writing talent worth developing, and he'd urged my to try submitting some short stories he had liked. If they had had any merit, his connections and recommendations might have ensured publication, but I couldn't do it. Every time I looked at them I made changes, and I knew I'd never be satisfied tomorrow with today's work. I didn't want to be a writer anyway. I put words to paper as a means of clarifying my thoughts, and from long-standing habit, I refused to share those thoughts with any but a very few people.

The description of the artists' retreat must have satisfied my mother, because she let me go without objection, and even drove me from our home in Delmar to the Plaza in Albany. There my luggage and I were transferred to Harris DeLyon's car for the drive up the Cape. A powerful local tycoon and crony of Cliff's, Harris and his wife Pam threw lavish parties, getting the right people together for the purpose of launching and advancing careers. Cliff and I had attended several of these last winter. The oldest of Harris and Pam's five children was my age, and still in high school. I always felt awkward when I ran into her in the kitchen or hallway at these parties. She'd look at me as if to say, "What are *you* doing *here*?"

Harris brought this same feeling out in me now, as he intimated subtly that I was too young and too naive for the crowd at Mary Bea's. Knowing his reputation as a lecher, I declined to respond with the objections he expected. His script would call for me to go out of my way to prove that I was a woman of the world.

Next he assured me that I could speak freely about my relationship with Cliff, since he knew all about it anyway. "In that case," I told him reasonably, "there's nothing to discuss."

"I can't figure you out," he admitted. "Are you a machinator? An opportunist? If you are, you can sure hide it. But what other reason would you have for hanging around Cliff? He's only held together with scotch tape and bobby pins, you know."

I fumed silently out my window, and when I didn't answer he looked sideways at me.

"Whew! Bet Cliff never saw you look so mad. You only turn on the charm for him? Well, sorry if you feel insulted, but what else can it be? He can't be such great shakes in bed. Or maybe you just don't know the difference. Is that it? Never had a boyfriend? Don't know what it's all about?"

"Is it inconceivable to you," I finally asked, "that Cliff and I could be just friends?"

"Oh, you poor dear! Cliff has plenty of friends his own age. Friends you couldn't possibly compete with in terms of intellectual stimulation. Do you really think he's going to spend his only vacation of the year with a friend—a child?"

"I don't know why the relationship should change suddenly. After all, I've known Cliff for over a year. I think I know what to expect from him."

"I hope for your sake you're right," Harris said. "But if you are, he's a bigger fool than I think he is."

The trip continued for several miles without conversation, and then he started in again. How many boyfriends had I had? What was the extent of my sexual experience? Controlling the impulse to tell him to mind his own business, I steered the conversation to his family. Pam and the children were already at the summer home in Orleans, and we were expected there for lunch. I found that Laurie, the oldest girl, would be going to Vassar this fall, but I evaded questions about my own school plans. There was not a thing about my life or my thoughts that I wished to share with this man.

Eventually, he gave up on conversation and turned off the highway onto a side road, where we wasted my time and my patience as he attempted to impose his weight on me, huffing and puffing. I extricated myself from his grasp, slid out from under his sweating bulk, and finally got out of the car, determined to walk to the nearest Greyhound station. I wasn't afraid of him, just insulted, and really weary of this type of scenario. I was a skinny girl, no *femme fatale*, and I looked more like a boy than a woman. Aside from his own curiosity, the only thing that could have excited him was my youth. He drove along beside me, cajoling me from his window, like a rejected high school romeo trying to talk his date back into the car. Finally he managed to convince himself that I wasn't worth the trouble, and to convince me that I might as well get back in and hug the door handle for the rest of the ride. The whole episode was so humdrum, it wouldn't even have made a good scandal for the season.

***

Pam waved to us from a hammock in the yard. Barefoot and in shorts, she got up to meet us. A glorious tan complemented her startling grey eyes and the silver streaks in her hair.

"I'd just about given up on you," she said. "The kids have already eaten."

"We got a late start," Harris lied, giving her shoulders a hug. I felt embarrassed, cheap, as I followed them into the house, and even more so as Laurie passed me, her eyes saying "Oh, you again." After washing up I joined Pam in the kitchen.

"Pam," I said, "there's no need for Harris to drive me all the way to Provincetown. If you could just help me get my luggage to the station, I'd rather take the bus."

"But that's silly! He's going up to Mary Bea's anyway!" She handed me a salad to put on the table.

At lunch I was quiet, looking down at my plate, not wanting to look at Harris across from me.

"Are you all right, dear?" Pam asked me, as she looked at her husband suspiciously.

"I put my hand on her knee, and she thought she was going to be raped," he said nonchalantly, helping himself to more potato salad.

"Oh Hare! You didn't!" She shook her head, chastising him affectionately. "You mustn't mind him, Joan," she told me. "He's just an old clown."

Did she know? Did this sort of thing happen all the time?

Later, as Pam and I did the dishes, Harris ate the leftovers and then cut a second piece of apple pie.

"He'll be a blimp if he keeps that up, won't he?" Pam said to me, laughing. Then she turned to him. "What time will you be home, hon?"

"Don't count on me for dinner, but I'll be home by bedtime." He patted her fanny and she looked up at him with a sparkle in her eye.

"Later!" he said, grabbing a handful of pretzels and stuffing them into his mouth as he walked out the door. Pam's eyes followed him adoringly and I watched in disbelief. *She loves this old buffoon. What can she possibly see in him?*

"Bye, Pam. Thanks for the lunch," I said, following Harris.

"You have a good vacation, Joan. See you in Albany!"

I was less apprehensive now about the remainder of the trip. In the car I remarked, "Pam's beautiful."

"She's getting fat."

"You should talk!"

"Hah! I guess I should." He laughed. "Yeah, Pam's a doll. Comfortable as an old shoe."

"That's not very complimentary."

"Well, you needn't entertain any illusions about your desirability. Do you think I'd prefer a child to Pam? I'm just going to Mary Bea's to work up an appetite."

"I thought Mary Bea's was an artists' retreat."

"Is that what Cliff told you? Well, I guess you could call it that, with a stretch of imagination. But artists have models, you know."

"Models? Life models?" I asked. "But Provincetown is a landscape artist's paradise."

"Oh my." He shook his head at me, laughing. "You really did fall out of some star, didn't you?"

* * *

At last we pulled into the driveway of a brown-shingled house, secluded above the busy life of the town.

"Now give me a little kiss to show there are no hard feelings." I turned my face away, and Harris said, "You're a silly girl and Cliff's welcome to you!"

We pulled the luggage out of the trunk and Cliff came to help us.

"Thanks for the ride," I said.

"It was nothing," he replied, setting suitcases on the ground. "I really mean that." He slapped Cliff on the back, saying "You really know how to pick 'em, old buddy," and then preceded us into the house, leaving us with the luggage.

Cliff asked "Whose idea was that? Harris driving you up?"

"He offered. My mother accepted. After all, he's a respectable married man. He'd treat me as he would his own daughter, wouldn't you think?"

"Are you all right? If he. . ."

"Sure I'm all right, except for the insult of listening to him all day. He's harmless enough, the old fart!"

"Must have been quite a trip! I never thought I'd hear you use an expression like that."

"I was inspired," I answered. Exasperated was more like it.

We entered the room through a dismal neglected kitchen. Congealed food in varying stages of decay was everywhere. It clung to a sinkful of dishes and stuck to the cutting board, counters, and stove top. A dingy fruit bowl contained three oozing black bananas, a rotten peach, and a community of fruit flies. Visible through the doorway, the next room was full of people and smoke and noise, explaining the collection of empty liquor bottles lined up on the kitchen floor.

"Ah, here's Mary Bea!" Cliff introduced me to a small dark-haired woman who gave me a sad, tired smile as she filled a bowl with ice cubes from the refrigerator. Someone called to Cliff and he rushed off with a hasty apology.

"Where shall I put my luggage?" I asked Mary Bea.

"Oh, anywhere you can find space."

"Isn't there a room available?"

She looked at me strangely as though trying to understand the meaning of my question. Leaving the kitchen with the ice cubes, she asked "Aren't you coming in?"

I started to follow her but something in the atmosphere made me prefer the kitchen. I stood in the doorway trying to define it. The difference between this party and those I had attended with Cliff last winter had nothing to do with the size of the crowd or the amount of liquor consumed. It was a matter of quality. I listened in on conversation that was entirely mindless, full of sarcastic wit. And these tanned voluptuous women were not beautiful, merely sexy. Compared with other women I had met through Cliff, they were lacking in charm and grace. I wondered if they could all be models. In spite of trite flattering phrases, the banter between the sexes here was a warlike game of one-upsmanship. These could be sophisticates only in the most archaic sense of the word.

Cliff was oblivious, interviewing a vacationing sculptor. And there was Harris, working up an appetite. He had been right about one thing. I *was* too young and naive for this crowd, and as out of place as my tailored linen suit.

Cliff returned, pocketing his ever-present note pad. This would be a working vacation for him.

"Come on in and get acquainted," he said, taking my arm.

"I don't think I'm going to stay, Cliff. I'd like to get down to town and find another place to stay before it gets dark."

"Oh, no! What's the matter? Are you worried about your room?"

"Partly."

"Joan, I told you the room would be no problem. When this party is over you'll have your choice of rooms. Just trust me. Please?"

"How many of these people live here?"

"Not many. Ten at most. Those are the people I want you to meet."

"Then it's not always like this?"

"No, not at all. You'll see tomorrow. It will be quiet, just like I told you."

"And this?" I swept my arm around the kitchen like a prima donna.

"As soon as the party's over. You'll see."

"Looks like it's been a long party."

"Come on now. I want you to meet some people."

"I'd like to change first."

"Well, let's put your luggage in my room for the time being."

Upstairs, we walked onto a large balcony with a row of doors. Cliff unlocked the first of these and swung it open, putting my suitcase inside.

"There you are! Make yourself comfortable. I'll be waiting downstairs."

The bedroom was clean at least, and the bed with its white-tufted spread looked inviting, reminding me how tired I was. I'd give the place a chance. I could always go somewhere else tomorrow. Opening my suitcase, I looked for something casual, and settled on a dirndle skirt, sleeveless shirt, and my sandals, their soles worn thin from last year's Provincetown sand. I took my clothes and towel and washcloth down the hall to the bathroom and found it almost as bad as the kitchen. Mary Bea needed some help in this house. No wonder she looked tired, trying to keep up with a constant turnover of guests, to say nothing of hostessing parties like this one. Maybe tomorrow I could give her a hand.

***

Downstairs, Cliff and I circulated and I became superficially acquainted with too many people. I didn't doubt that there were some among them I'd enjoy knowing, but that wasn't what I'd come up the Cape for. I wanted the sun and sand and sea.

The room was stuffy and so crowded we were elbow to elbow, whether standing or sitting. Next to me a woman was asking her companion of the moment, "What do you do?"

"I'm a dilettante," he answered.

"Really! How long have you been doing this?"

"Long enough to be good at it. What do you do?"

"That remains for you to find out!" she laughed raucously. "But I'll tell you this: I'm very good at it."

I pulled at Cliff's sleeve to get his attention. "I'd like to walk around outside for a while, Cliff. Wouldn't you like to get some air?"

"Tomorrow we'll go to the beach," he said.

"I'm going out now while there's still some light."

I explored around behind the house, wandering through dune grass, beach plum, bayberry, and scrubby pines. I found a cat, or she found me. She seemed to want me to follow her, going ahead of me for a few feet, then coming back to circle around me before going on again. She led me to a small shed where she disappeared through an opening between two boards. A chorus of tiny "mew's" welcomed her. She brought a kitten out, carrying it in her mouth, and lay down in front of me to nurse it, telling me the only way she could that she needed food.

"I'll see what I can do," I told her and went back to the house.

The sun was going down when I went inside. I stood in the middle of the kitchen wondering what I could find to feed the cat. The screen door behind me slammed and before I had a chance to turn around, two hands were over my breasts pulling on me. I stiffened and pushed the hands away, then turned to face a fair blond man in his twenties.

"I'm sorry," he said. "That was a very sneaky pass. Can you forgive me?" He looked very contrite and just a little drunk.

"You sort of took me by surprise," I told him.

"That was my intention."

"Do you live here?"

"Yes. Bob Steen's the name. Would you like something to eat?" He spoke with precise Harvard enunciation.

"Well—that's the best idea I've heard since I got here! But first, there's a cat with kittens out in back. Is there something here I could feed her?"

He took a can of cat food from the cupboard and handed it to me with a can opener.

"Just reach inside the shed and you'll find a dish."

He cleared a space on the counter by condensing the clutter, put down a clean plate and assembled sandwich makings. I ran out to feed the cat.

Cliff was in the kitchen, too, when I returned.

"There you are!" he exclaimed. "I was about to go out and look for you."

"You must be Joan," Steen said to me as he sliced the sandwiches in half. To Cliff he said, "I made a pass at her before I knew she was your girl. We're going to have something to eat."

"Take good care of her, Steen," Cliff said, waving as he returned to the living room.

I gave some thought to Steen's remark to Cliff. This was the implication of what he'd said: that a man could treat an unattached woman any way he pleased, but an attached woman was a different story. So he would have respect for what he considered to be another man's property, but would have no respect for the woman herself. I was sobered by the thought, and determined not to forget it, because I knew there had to be some way to use this depressing knowledge to my advantage.

Steen handed me an unwieldy sandwich consisting of ham, cheese, olives, tomato, and lettuce, a meal in itself. I wrapped a napkin around it to contain it and we took our sandwiches to the stairs, watching the crowd, which had dwindled a little in the time I had been gone.

"What do you do, Joan?" Steen asked.

"I'm a dilettante," I mimicked.

"Oh, very good!"

I started to tell him I wasn't Cliff's girl but decided to let it go, reminding myself that there were benefits to the appearance of attachment.

The night wore on and I could hardly keep my eyes open. Cliff's coordination was suffering. He usually handled his liquor well, but tonight he had overdone it.

"I've never seen you like this before," I told him.

"I'm not driving," he explained.

"Cliff, what can I do? I'm dead on my feet and I've got to lie down somewhere."

"Here." He handed me a key. "Take my room."

"I can't take *your* room."

"Call it yours then, if it helps. By the time I'm ready to go to bed there'll be another."

"What about your gear?" I asked.

"No, I'm not going to move it now. That would be too confusing. Just go ahead and get some sleep and I'll see you in the morning. Or in the afternoon, as the case may be."

Too tired to object, I went upstairs, locked myself in and went to sleep in my clothes.

Some time later I woke to find Cliff climbing into bed beside me. This was not the Cliff I knew and trusted, not the Cliff who had been like a father to me. And now *this* was no paternal embrace. I pushed at him, trying to free myself, feeling furiously betrayed. My protector had become a stranger.

"Stay," he was saying. "Don't fight me." But I had gotten loose and was reaching for my sandals, stuffing them into a tote bag with my towel.

"You can't!" he said. "You can't leave me like this!"

"Oh yes I can!"

I ran barefoot down the stairs, still hearing him call, "Joan! Come back!"

He'll wake the whole house, I thought, but that didn't bother me at all. I went through the filthy kitchen and out into the damp sand, gray, just before dawn. It agonized me to admit it to myself, but Harris had been right about Cliff. And about me, too. I was exactly the naïve, stubborn girl he'd described. I looked at myself in the pre-dawn light, and then looked up at the sky, thinking to myself: *Joan, you really did fall out of some star, didn't you?*

Chapter Three

At a diner in the center of town I stopped, put my sandals on, and ordered breakfast. While the eggs fried I brushed my teeth in the rest room, glad my toothbrush had remained packed in my tote.

Afterward I started down the road to the beach without a thought about Cliff. Any affection or allegiance I had felt toward him had been erased in just one moment. I'd pick up my things later.

The sun was up and the road was deserted. I sang to the morning, making up my own words and tune as I walked. Today I'd get a room at the house where I'd stayed last year. The aroma of Portuguese sausage and lobster drifted perpetually upward from the kitchen there, and there was always fresh linen. I'd be fine.

* * *

There was no one on the beach at this early hour. I plunged into the water in my underwear and then ran on the hard wet sand to dry myself before dressing. In the afternoon the crowds came, and I started back to town by way of the sand. Suddenly I ran into Cliff and Steen.

"Where are you going?" Cliff called.

"To Grace's, where I stayed last year."

"Well, let me give you a lift." He pulled his pants on over trunks.

"Sure," I said. I wasn't going to hold a grudge on such a beautiful day. The three of us trudged through the sand toward the road, Steen walking ahead, purposely, I thought, to give us a chance to talk. I hoped his consideration would prove unnecessary, but I was not that lucky.

"About last night," Cliff began. "I'm really sorry. I didn't even know who you were."

"Oh, you didn't know who I was? Cliff, didn't you call after me by name as I ran from the room?" I asked. "I don't want to talk about it," I added decisively. "I don't even want to think about it."

"You can forget about it then?"

"I already have. I've forgotten everything. Last winter, all the things we've done together, everything."

It was amazing. He didn't even look the same to me. It had always given me such a lift to see him, to anticipate the conversation, the companionship. I had delighted in the sound of his voice, in his habits, his idiosyncracies, the sight and sound of him. Now, since last night, he looked like any other old man I might pass on the street without noticing. He had become an object, the existence of which had no significance in my life.

We all got into the front seat. Cliff was silent as we drove downtown, but as he parked in front of The Mayflower he said, "Come in for a minute. There's a colorful local character I want you to meet."

"All right, but just for a minute. I don't want to delay too long in getting to Grace's."

"You have time," he said. "I just saved you some. What would you like to drink?"

"Ginger ale, I guess." I slid into the red upholstered booth next to Cliff, facing the door, Steen across from us.

"Ginger ale!"

"I'm under age," I reminded him. "You seem to have forgotten. Who is this you want me to meet?"

"Manny Zoro, a Portuguese fisherman. He owns a scallop fishing boat. Should be coming in any minute now. They usually dock about four o'clock."

We watched the door as blue-clad fishermen straggled into the bar, separated from the booths by a shoulder-high partition.

"His boat should be in now. That's one of his men." Cliff inclined his head toward a blue-shirted figure standing in the doorway. Uncomprehending, but entirely stricken, I stared at the figure.

Dark as a gypsy, longish black curls damp with sea spray, this was a fisherman to be sure, yet wholly set apart, as distinctive as a rose in a potato field. His onyx eyes darted about the room with expectancy, intensity. It was as if a French nobleman had stepped out of a classical portrait to spend a day on a scallop dragger. Looking again, I saw a pirate, a young prince, an elf, an Adonis. Contained in him, radiating from him, was a singular quality that pervaded my mind like a song from far away. An instant of recognition echoed some moment in eternity when all was, or would be, innocence. I felt as though I had just set down a burden I had carried too long. I held my breath, dazzled by the sunlight behind him, until our eyes met and he came to sit down across from me.

"Cathy!" he cried breathlessly. "Where have you been? I've been searching for you all over the dunes!" I drank in the hint of a smile at the corners of his mouth, a glint that hid in the sadness of his eyes, and I knew he expected me to understand this riddle.

"Joan," Steen said, "Bill Cannastra. Or Heathcliff when he prefers."

"Heathcliff? Ah," I said.

"I think I see him now, at the bar!" Cliff cried.

"Who?" Bill asked.

"Manny Zoro," I told him.

"Oh, you want to see Manny?" Bill took my hand and we went around one end of the partition while Cliff went around the other.

"Manny!" Bill said. "I want you to meet my *galinha*. She's coming with me on the boat tomorrow. Did I say that right, Manny? Gah-leen-ya?"

"You say it right, Bill," Manny said affectionately.

Cliff stood there speechless for a moment, then turned and walked away. When we returned to the booth, both he and Steen were gone.

Bill and I sat there for some time, gazing at each other, wordlessly exchanging information and laughing now and then. I was filled with the most wonderful, ethereal feeling. *Here is a friend,* I was sure, *who will accept me as I am. Here is where I can stop pretending. Here is… my tool for obtaining all the knowledge I am meant to have.*

Finally it grew dark and Bill stood up. "Come," he said.

"Where?"

"To my house." We ran through town hand in hand, out onto the dunes, and finally to a little board house sitting in the sand against a dark sky filled with stars and a crescent moon.

"Slowly," he cautioned as we crossed the threshold. Then I saw why. The living room contained a lake, which reflected the stars and moon from the open windows. He didn't turn on the lights.

"Around this way." He led me around the dry edges to the far side of the lake. Fortunately for the eight-foot row of record albums on the floor along the wall, the floor slanted toward the door.

"Beautiful!" I said.

"Glad you like it. I rather do myself." He put the sofa cushions at the edge of the lake and asked, "Don't you think Handel's 'Water Music' would be appropriate?"

I agreed and he put the first record on. We took off our shoes and dipped our feet into the water. All night long we listened to music and drank zinfandel, passing the bottle back and forth, and throwing our cigarette butts into the lake, where they disappeared.

At the first gray light in the sky Bill said, "Time for the boat!," and we stood up to go out the door. There was just enough light now to see the lake for what it really was. The drip pan under the ice box had overflowed, running into the living room from the kitchen. The stars were gone. Cigarette butts were in their place, and we could see the floorboards through the dirty water.

"Is it ruined?" he asked.

"No," I answered. "It was magic." Then we ran again down the sand road, through town and onto the wharf. Bill stopped at the head of a rope ladder.

"Wait," he said. "Take your skirt and do like this." He pantomimed pulling a skirt between his legs like a diaper. I complied and followed him down the ladder.

"Bunch of dirty sailors on this boat," he said. At the bottom of the ladder, on deck, he took me past the 'dirty sailors,' introducing me again as his *galinha*. Then we went down to the galley, where he made coffee, explaining that he was the cook. After he had taken coffee and donuts up to the crew, we sat down to our own.

"What does that mean? *Galinha*?" I asked him.

"It means that you're my girl so they'll leave you alone."

An echo of yesterday's lesson. I wanted to ask Bill about it. "Why is it," I asked, "that it's always open season on single women?"

"I guess it's the price women pay for freedom. Don't you know?"

"So I can't be respected unless I am somebody's girl? But if I'm somebody's girl, I can't be free?"

Bill smiled. "When women are protected they are respected.

The only way a woman can fully be respected is to be somebody's wife. But there are always those who run around freely and do everything just as they like. That's what kind of a woman you are, Cathy!"

I thought it over. "I'll give up the respect, for the time being," I decided. "I'd rather be nobody's wife."

He went up to get the dishes, and as we did them he said "I meant to thank you for not talking over the music last night."

"It was glorious! A glorious night," I said.

Bill put a huge pot on the fire and started the beef browning for a pot roast. I diced onions and green peppers while he peeled potatoes, urging me, "Hurry, sweetie. There's something else glorious coming up and I don't want us to miss it."

Once we had everything simmering, he took a bottle from under the sink, had a few quick gulps, and replaced it. Then we went up on deck. I asked him, "Do you drink all the time?"

"Yes," he said. "All the time."

We were heading out beyond Race Point now, full speed ahead. Standing at the prow, which cut the sea, sending salty spray back into our faces, we shouted and laughed over the noise of the engines. A red glow appeared ahead of us on the horizon.

"Now watch!" Bill shouted. He pulled me close beside him as the red ball of sun exploded out of the sea, setting the mist and clouds on fire, and making rainbows in the spray. I felt a low "Boom!" resonate all through me.

"You heard it, didn't you?" he yelled.

"Yes! Or felt it! Is it real?"

"Real enough! I still haven't decided if it's an illusion or not. But isn't it wonderful?"

"Magnificent! Is it like this every day?"

"Just about! It's worth having this job, just for that. But no one else here sees it."

It was strange to be shouting so loud and yet barely be heard.

The rest of the crew clustered in small groups, smoking and shouting their own important matters, oblivious to ours and unaware of the spectacular display the sun had just put on for us.

"There's never anyone to share it with, and it makes me sad to watch it alone," he said into my ear. "But to have you see it and feel it with me! What is it that makes it so wonderful?"

"I think it's love," I said, surprised to hear it come out of my own mouth. I added, "But not just an ordinary personal love. It's bigger, it's like... singing hymns of praise in church. That kind of love. Do you know what I mean?"

"Oh, sweetie! Yes! I do know what you mean. If we can keep it on that level it will be so good. But I'm so afraid we'll do something to soil it before the day's over."

"No, we won't," I insisted. "We won't soil it."

"Then we can be innocents? Babes in the woods? You'll be my little sister?"

"And you'll be my little brother."

We leaned against the rail, smiling at each other, sea spray mixing with tears until no one would have known we were crying and we wouldn't have cared anyway. It was the first time I had cried since I was twelve, but these were tears of relief and gratitude, emotions opened by finally finding a friend with whom all pretending was possible, yet to whom I need not pretend.

The boat had slowed down now, ten miles past the point. Manny was feeling his way around, intuitively finding the best spot to let down the metal net called a "rake." He made his decision and we bobbed around quietly while the rake was let down from the winch. Once it was all the way down we got up speed, dragging the rake across the ocean floor for miles, until it was pulled up by means of a crank. Bill worked the winch and as the scallops came up, all hands went to work cutting the meat out of the shell, filling big net bags with the white morsels. The bags were then hung from the side of the boat to keep the precious haul cool in the water.

The name of the boat, the *Piraga*, painted on the side, made me think of a pirogue, a canoe-shaped boat. But this boat was a converted catamaran, and I asked Manny, "What does *Piraga* mean?"

"It means poor fisherman if I don't get a better catch than this!" he yelled, as the crew laughed.

Bill and I went below to check on the pot roast while the boat headed back out again. Between the wine and lack of sleep, Bill ruined the dinner. He went wild with seasoning, pouring whole bottles of wine and jars of mustard and pickle relish into the pot, adding an institutional-size can of stuffed olives for good measure. The complaints at mealtime were colorful, spattered with insults only sailors could invent, and Manny threatened to put Bill ashore.

"Like a son I love you, Bill, but you make me crazy with these things. You make my crew sick! What I'm going to do with you? Hah?" He looked at me. "Can you cook?"

"Yes! Yes! She can!" Bill insisted.

"Then you cook!" Manny ordered me. "Bill goes ashore. I can't keep him no more."

"No good, Manny," one of the crew objected. "She can't man the winch. We lose one hand that way."

"And I can't stay on the boat without Bill," I added.

So it was settled that Bill would work on deck and I'd work in the galley. Each of us would be paid one share instead of Bill getting his former two shares.

Bill was drunkenly ecstatic. He danced along the rail, lost his balance and went overboard. Fortunately, the boat wasn't moving, and we managed to get him hauled aboard before Manny knew anything about it.

Chapter Four

I came to know why Bill called the galley "Hades." Between the heat of the engines and the gas fire of the stove, I couldn't stand a stitch of clothing beyond my bathing suit. In the days that followed, the crew stretched Manny's credulity with inventive reasons to have to come below, but I was too busy and too distracted by the heat to care. As soon as the meal was finished and the dishes done, I'd notify Manny of my intention to go over for a swim, so he wouldn't get up speed and leave me behind. With a rope tied around my waist, in case of sharks, and the whole Atlantic for my bathtub, I'd wash my hair while the crew gawked. Then I'd go up on the cabin roof to sun myself and gawk at them while they worked, their brown muscular backs glistening with sweat. I enjoyed being both the exhibitionist and the voyeur. They seemed to appreciate my cooking, and I appreciated their tolerance about having a woman on board. Not one of them ever gave me any serious trouble. Because just to keep matters at a certain level of respect, we never let go the appearance that I was Bill Cannastra's *galinha.*

***

Our day off finally arrived, and Bill and I made plans to gather periwinkles to put in a spaghetti sauce, but first there were some things to be done around the house. I did the laundry in the bathtub, kneeling on the broken linoleum, homely but homey in its decrepit cleanliness.

A week's worth of laundry was nothing for posterity, but it would be some sort of progress at least. My reward would be the sense of accomplishment I'd savor, hanging the clean things in the sun, and I anticipated it as I carried the laundry basket outside to the line. Bill was on the roof pushing around the TV antenna, and he called down.

"Want some help hanging that up?"

"No," I answered. "I like doing it!"

As I pinned the first towel to the line, Cliff's old gray Ford stopped in front of the house, and he and Steen got out. I was ready to welcome them until Cliff explained his mission. He considered himself responsible for me and could not let me stay with this "maniac," this "sexually depraved madman." If I refused to listen to reason he'd call my mother.

"Oh, you will!" I was indignant. "Be sure to tell her what happened last Friday night when you're describing the sexual depravity part!"

"I explained about that," he said.

"I know. You didn't know who I was. Well, you listen, Cliff. Bill always knows who I am, so there's no need for your concern."

"I don't know what's come over you, Joan, to take up with a common fisherman."

"Now wait a minute!" I had an answer, but Steen jumped in with his own.

"You know how it is, Cliff. Youth to youth. Belly to belly."

Bill jumped up and down on the roof laughing, patting his

stomach. "Belly to belly? Belly to belly! Ho ho! *Soul* to *soul*! What do you think of that, old man?"

I couldn't resist telling Cliff, "Bill's taking his vacation as a fisherman. Actually he's an attorney. A New York lawyer!"

"Is this true?" Cliff asked Steen.

"Very true, very true," Steen answered.

I turned away from them, and the laundry found its way onto the line, but I'd lost all pleasure in hanging it up. Cliff had cast a dark shadow over the day, Bill's and my day. I went into the house without another word, slamming the door angrily behind me. Bill was unusual, unpredictable, even outlandish... but a "maniac"? A "sexually depraved madman"? Bill had already told me he was bisexual, and I knew sometimes he despaired and felt disgust at his own behavior, but all he'd ever been to me was a caring big brother. Were his sweetness and his decency that hard to see? From the window I saw Bill go up to the car and speak to Steen. Then he turned with a wave and ran into the house, laughing as the car took off down the road.

"His concern is not fatherly!" he said, coming in the door. "He acts like a woman scorned. What did you do to him anyway?"

"It's what I didn't do. I wonder if he'll call my mother."

"What good would that do him?"

"Probably none, but it could upset my mother. And for no reason." I sat down on the couch to put on my sandals. "What crime are we committing? What could be more prosaic than this?"

"People make judgments based on their own experience," he said. "How would you, as an observer, interpret a situation like this?"

"What right would I have to interpret? I've always hated that! It makes me angry when anyone presumes to guess my motives or analyze me. I'd avoid doing it to someone else."

"But suppose one of the parties was important to you. Let's say you had some concern for the safety of that party."

"Well... I hope I'd allow for the possibility that it wasn't what it seemed to be."

"Good girl!" He seemed to twinkle at me.

"But Cliff isn't concerned for my safety, Bill. As you noticed, he acts like a rejected woman. And if he really cared, he could get to know you better. The facts of the situation aren't that hard to come by. He's being spiteful!"

"Careful. You're guessing at his motives," Bill teased.

"And I don't really care what they are. I just don't want him meddling in my life." I sighed and planted my feet solidly on the floor. "Let's go get those periwinkles!"

"I'm ready," he said. "My trunks are under my jeans."

"So's my suit. Let's go!"

He took two small net bags from the kitchen and we set off for the bay, walking slowly, no need to hurry now that we were outside on this perfect day. I looked back at my morning's labor, billowing softly in the sunshine against the blue backdrop of the cloudless sky. Now I looked forward to the pleasure of bringing it in later, clean and fresh smelling.

"You know, sweetie," Bill continued on a subject I wished to forget, "it might be of some value to you to understand Cliff's motives."

"I don't care about his motives," I reiterated, shaking my head. "I don't want to understand them."

"You don't want him to call your mother though, and if you could evaluate his reasons you could better predict his actions. Maybe even prevent them."

"How?" I asked, my interest kindled.

"You could start by imagining yourself in his position."

"Impossible! There's nothing in my experience that approximates that position. How can I imagine things I've never felt?"

"You've never sorrowed over the loss of a friend?"

"No. Not that either," I admitted. "But that's not the position I thought you meant."

"What did you think I was talking about?"

"I thought you meant, the position that led to his loss of my friendship. Or friendship as we knew it. We were really quite close last winter, you know, Bill."

"And in spite of that closeness you could shut him out of your life because of something you didn't understand?"

"Yes," I answered simply and sadly.

The tide was out, leaving behind a playground of wet sand dotted with sky-colored oblongs of sea water. We hung our clothes on nails jutting from the wharf pilings and stuffed the net bags into our suits. After a quick swim we dried and walked in the sun along sand bars, splashing through rivulets and pools as we gathered the periwinkles.

"How do you get them out of the shells?" I asked.

"With a pin! I'll show you when we get home. We'll have *spaghettini littorini*."

"What's that?"

"The Latin name for these little things." He held one up and defined it. "Of the genus *littorina*."

I repeated it to myself several times.

"My grandfather used to do that," I told Bill. "He gave me the Latin names for plants. And when I didn't know the meaning of a new word, he'd take it apart and show me the Latin root."

"He did you a favor. It's a good habit to get into."

"Did you study Latin?"

"Oh yes, it's essential for law students. But it all began with a childhood of Latin Masses." He stopped in his tracks and began without announcement, without a trace of self-consciousness, to sing a Mass. I heard the clear innocent voice of the choirboy he must have been. "That's *Vidi Aquam*," he said.

"You were a choirboy?"

"Of course! In Schenectady." He repeated it, delighting in the name. "Schen-ec-ta-dy. Have you heard of it?"

"Sure! Schenectady is right next to Albany. We've lived in Albany County since '43."

Our bags filled, we returned to the spot where we had left our clothes and sat on the dry sand to have a smoke. Bill's hands shook as he lit his cigarette, and his face showed the effect of last night's alcoholic extremes. He hadn't had a thing to drink so far today.

"You all right?" I asked him.

"Not quite," he said. "But I'm going to hold off till dinner. I want to take you to meet some friends later and I don't want to be too impossibly smashed."

He sat in ill-fitting trunks with his knees up, his genitals resting on the sand. His lack of concern made it seem entirely natural that they should be exposed there. Freed from a sexual context, there was no reason this part of the anatomy should be any less ordinary or beautiful than the next.

"I keep forgetting to get a lemon squeezer and some lemons," he mused. "Someone told me that if I drink large quantities of lemon juice, it will be easier not to drink on those rare occasions when I wish to be sober."

"I'll remember to get them tomorrow when I pick up the boat provisions."

"That will be great, sweetie! But I should warn you against shouldering an alcoholic's responsibilities."

"I wouldn't dream of such a thing," I assured him. "I'm just remembering something for a forgetful friend."

Bill's drinking was cyclic. If he slept at all, the moment he woke was the zenith of sobriety. From that point on through the day, he usually drank methodically until he passed out, and passing out was equivalent to bed time. He could not sleep otherwise. He didn't need to be shown the seriousness of his drinking problem, any more than a man preparing to jump from a roof needed to be made aware of what would happen when he hit the ground. Bill was intelligent, and he could see with sadness and with clarity all he needed to know about his psychological state and precipitous condition. What he needed was a reason, any reason, not to jump.

"Who are these people we're going to visit tonight?" I asked.

"Bruce and Mary. They're brother and sister and they really mean a lot to me, as you do, sweetie. I hope... I think... you'll like each other."

I looked forward to the evening. Anyone important enough to Bill to inspire a whole day's sobriety would be worth meeting.

"You don't like my cheap red wines," he noted. "Let's get something you like to go with dinner. Then I won't have to drink alone."

"Maybe a sauterne?" I suggested. I took our clothes down from the pilings and threw his to him. "But no matter how much I like the wine, I don't enjoy being drunk."

"Ah, but you've found other ways to obliterate the pain," he said as we dressed.

"How do you know that?"

"I can see it. There's no suffering in your eyes."

"I don't feel pain. I've never felt it. There is a chemical imbalance in my body that doesn't let the pain sensation reach my brain at all. You know, Bill, I don't even let the dentist use novocaine on me."

"That's interesting, sweetie. And it shows on you. But there's more than that."

"Yes," I conceded. "More than that, I'm like a blank page with nothing written on it."

"There's a lot written on it, but not suffering."

"But that's the way I feel—blank! You talk about the loss of a friend. I don't know anything about that. There are so many things I don't know about and can't empathize with. I'm in an isolated position, Bill. It's comfortable enough but it leaves huge gaps in my understanding."

"I see that, too. That's why I thought it would be good for you to put yourself in Cliff's shoes. As sort of an exercise. You don't feel isolated from me though, do you?"

"No, not at all."

"I wonder if you could turn your back on *me*, if I did something you didn't understand." The intensity in his eyes demanded an answer.

"No, I couldn't. Even if I didn't understand," I answered sincerely.

"Why not? Why doesn't the isolation include me?"

"I've been thinking about that." I struggled to articulate the reason, but couldn't, even to myself. "It's impossible to put into words, Bill! I could almost draw you a picture more easily, because I can see it better than I can verbalize it. And it might sound a little crazy to you."

"No, no, sweetie! Nothing you could say would sound crazy. Please try to tell me how you see it, because I've been thinking about it too."

"Well," I began, "can you imagine being related to something that existed before we did? And would exist even if we didn't? Something abstract—a reference point. Which I guess may or may not have physical dimensions."

"How do you mean, 'physical'?"

"Measurable. Like us, like all matter."

"Hmm. You mean a constant, or a parameter, of some sort," he suggested.

"I'm not sure. Could our parameter be part of another. . ." I couldn't finish that idea and approached it another way. "Could it exist in one kind of space while we existed in another?" I thought it sounded a little crazy myself, but Bill looked thoughtful.

"Yes, it could!" He considered. "Think of a pendulum. It makes a circle with its trajectory, right?"

"Right!" I said.

"In a pendulum, you only see the circle as a part of the physical clock itself, within physical space. But the circle, the idea of the circle, exists apart from the physical space. Is that what you mean?"

"It's exactly what I mean, Bill!" I was excited that he understood. "We could be incomplete. We could be the imperfect manifestation of an idea. The idea's in one kind of reality or space, but we're in this imperfect world."

He smiled. "Have you read Plato, sweetie?"

I admitted that I hadn't.

"You have a treat in store," he promised. "Plato talked about mathematical forms as ideas that are eternal and complete. He said the form and law of all triangles is perfect, even if there never were any triangles in the physical world. Ideas remain unchanged even if all the objects to which they correspond are destroyed."

I wanted to know more. "Does this apply to humans, too? What does Plato say about mankind?"

"He says that men are born and die, but Man survives. Only the soul is real, it gives form to matter and beings, according to an ideal. So you see, you're not crazy, sweetie. You're in good company."

I spun around in delight, smiling back at the trail of our footprints in the sand, then turned and raced ahead of Bill on the beach.

**

In the package store, we dripped sea water from our periwinkle bags as we pondered the selection of an appropriate wine. Bill extolled the virtues of one and apprised me of the shortcomings of another, like the connoisseur he was. For my uneducated palate, one wine would suffice as well as the next, as long as it wasn't too sweet. We settled for a New York sauterne. I handed Bill my periwinkles and took the wine package, on the small chance that if I carried it he would leave it unopened till we got home. I was ashamed of my attempted subterfuge the minute we left the store.

"Hand me the wine, sweetie," Bill commanded. At the sound of my sigh he added, "And don't try to assume responsibility for me."

I was silent and looked guiltily down at the road.

"All right?" he asked.

"All right," I answered, chagrined. It was the last time I'd try anything like that. I walked ahead of him until he spoke again.

"Are you a virgin, sweetie?" he asked.

"No," I answered, puzzled. "Why do you ask?"

"You walk like you're not aware of being a woman. I've noticed it before. Like an innocent young girl."

"Awkward?" I asked.

"Yes, a little."

"It could be two things. One, I've had a number of injuries to my left leg. Broken bones, mostly, and polio affected it slightly when I was very young. And two, I don't know what... awareness of being a woman is supposed to feel like. I guess I'm probably not aware of anything other than the problems it presents. I really wish I were a boy at times."

"So do I," he said. "At times."

We walked silently while I tried to figure that one out.

"Do you like Mozart?" Bill asked.

"Oh, Bill, you make me confess my ignorance. I love *The*

Marriage of Figaro, but this morning when I was straightening up the place I had a good look at your record collection, and you have Mozart I've never heard."

"We'll put *The Magic Flute* on then, while the spaghetti sauce is cooking. You'll like that."

At home, we dumped the periwinkles into the sink to wash the sand out, and while Bill went to put on the first of the records, I got out the onions, green peppers, garlic, and other things I knew he'd want for the sauce. As I awaited instructions, Bill suddenly called out from the other room in alarm.

"What did you *do* in here?"

"What do you mean?" I ran into the room.

"What have you done to my records?"

"I just put them in order," I told him, wondering if I had broken any.

"In *order*? In alphabetical order? Oh, no, sweetie. Look at this. Bartok is a modern and belongs way up here at this end. Music has to be arranged chronologically."

"Oh! I'm sorry." I looked down, blushing. "I guess I've given you a big job, Bill, because I wouldn't know where to begin putting them back."

"You will," he said, laughing at the look on my face. He took a book from the shelf, and I made a mental note not to rearrange those either. "You'll find that every composer is listed in this book. You can arrange all the albums according to date of composition."

"Now?" I feared my cooking lesson had been canceled.

"No, not now, silly sweetie. We've got a dinner to cook!"

Cooking with Bill was a festive exercise, a great production. I was the assistant to the chef as we bustled about, kitcheneering, filling the room with steam and aroma. He kept me busy slicing this, dicing that, stirring something else, all instructions softly given as the strains of music gave depth and elegance to the hour. Outside the screen door, I learned how to pull the periwinkles out, and we left the shells to break down in the sand and carried a bowlful of delicious protein inside to add to the simmering sauce. Then it was time to boil the spaghetti, just long enough, *al dente*. What fun it was to test the strands by throwing them against the wall!

"Mine stuck!" I cried gleefully, ready to eat.

"So did mine!" Bill pointed to the Rita Hayworth poster left by a previous tenant. A worm of spaghetti curled over her thigh. We consulted by eye contact and agreed without a word that we had enough spaghetti to waste some. The next few minutes were spent in splattering the poster and laughing at the results. Finally we dished up and took our plates to the living room to enjoy what was absolutely the best spaghetti dinner I had ever tasted.

In excellent spirits born of good food, wine, music and laughter, we set off for Bruce's house. Bill announced our arrival with a brief knock at the open door and walked in. A pale delicate-looking girl with light blond hair and blue eyes lay on a cot on her side, knees bent to hold a pillow against her abdomen.

"Mary," Bill said softly, "this is Cathy."

"No!" she cried petulantly, and threw her pillow at him. "*Not* Cathy!"

Bill went to the other side of the room, and only then did I notice a slender young man with exactly the same coloring as Mary. Bill spoke to him for a few minutes while I regarded Mary, realizing finally that I must be staring at her as she was staring at me. We were like children sizing each other up. Bill had hoped we would like each other, but she had rejected me. What was my next move supposed to be? I considered leaving and waiting outside, and was about to do just that when Mary spoke.

"Those are pretty." She was not quite looking at me and I

couldn't imagine what she was referring to, until she touched her ear, her gaze fixed just off my face.

"Oh! My earrings," I finally deduced. I took them off and in a gesture so hypocritical I couldn't believe my own action, I offered the tiny turquoises to her.

"They would be pretty on you," I suggested, my hand outstretched. She made no move to take them, so I set them on the table beside her.

Bruce and Bill now came to join us, Bill to stand with me at the foot of the cot and Bruce to stand beside his sister. I was struck by the contrast of their delicate fair-haired paleness to our rugged dark-haired brownness. Mary began to rock and moan, and she looked to me as if she must be in pain.

I looked with alarm at Bill. "Should we do something for her?"

"No, nothing," he said. "Nothing can be done. It happens all the time."

On the dark road as we walked back to our house, Bill went unsteadily ahead, zigzagging from one side of the street to the other. He must have had quite a bit to drink in the short time we had been at Bruce's. He stopped in front of the house, but as I approached he said "I don't want to go in yet. Let's go down to the 'C' House for a while."

"No, I'm going to bed as soon as I take the laundry in. You go ahead if you want."

"You won't... come with me?" I could hear the pain and pleading in his voice, and I would have given in had it not been for his previous sober advice.

"No. I'm not coming with you."

"I don't... want to go... *alone!* You have to... come *with* me!" His eyes were wild, unseeing, and his manner and speech were unlike anything I had seen or heard before in all his drunkenness. In his state of mind, I thought, he might do something *really* outlandish. Yet if I went with him, I'd be setting a precedent that wouldn't do either of us any good.

"I'm going to stay here, Bill."

"Then *stay!* You filthy *bitch!* I don't *want* you with me. You're a *miscreant!* A living *abortion!* And *filthy!* Go *away!* I don't want to *see* you!"

I was numbed and shocked by the intensity of his insults. I knew I shouldn't take the vilification personally, but the direct way he hurled his words at me made it impossible to be strong under them. My legs weak, I went toward the house, stopping to take down the laundry, frustrated that I could still find no pleasure in the armload of sweet clean freshness. Bill stood in the road, still shouting invectives as I went inside. I shivered, remembering his question about "if I did something you didn't understand."

I folded the meaningless laundry, put everything away but my long flannel nightgown, and went upstairs to bed.

Moments later the door slammed and Bill shouted hoarsely.

"Cathy! Cathy! Where are you? Are you *here?*"

His steps came unevenly up the stairs. I heard him lurch through my doorway, and in the moonless dark he groped toward my bed, finding me, feeling my face, talking to me in that hesitant staccato pattern I had heard earlier.

"I didn't mean... please... *please* don't... *ever*... don't *listen* to me when... when I'm. . .*Cathy!*... I'm just, just very... *oblique!* I didn't say... say those things... to *you!* To *myself!* You're sort of... you're my *self*... my *mother!*"

He wasn't crying but the sound... of sobs was in the sudden intake of breath as he spoke. The inner torment came out in desperate shouts. He lifted my head and shoulders and sat down cradling me in his arms like a baby.

"You mustn't... mustn't worry... mustn't care... mustn't need me at all. Very... sort of *tenuous! All* of it. We come... and *go*. For all we *know!* I need... people tonight... and noise. You were right... not to come. And now... now you sleep. Sleep... good sweet Cathy. You won't... won't leave me?"

"No, I won't. It's all right, Bill."

He lay me down on the bed and covered me, saying, "Till the morning then... and the boat." And then he sang, in the Ink Spots' arrangement:

"For all we know we may never meet again.

"We come and go like the ripples on a stream.

"So. . ." His voice broke with that sobbing sound. He kissed my eyelids and went out, exiting with:

"Tomorrow may never come,

"For all we know."

I was shaken. Devastated! Reason wanted no part of the moment. My impulse was to get up and run after him. But to what end? To augment the audience for his self-destructive performance? It would make no difference in his behavior if I were there. I'd never seen him ranting like this before.

What had I told Cliff? "Bill always knows who I am." Then why was I "Cathy" when he was drunk and "sweetie" when he was sober? Never "Joan," even when he had introduced me to Mary. Had Mary once played Cathy to Bill's Heathcliff? If she had, she certainly didn't seem to consider me worthy of superseding her.

I thought sleep would never come, and when it finally did, my dreams were full of anger and shouts and cries.

Chapter Five

After docking the next afternoon, Bill and I separated where the wharf meets Commercial Street. I needed to take care of some errands, and Bill went to the Mayflower with friends. Bob Steen was in the post office when I went in to buy some stamps, and we walked out together, talking of this and that, nothing very important. He accompanied me, first to the New York Store where I remembered to get Bill's lemon squeezer, and then to the butcher's and grocer's to pick up the week's boat provisions and lemons.

"I have to take this stuff down to the boat," I told him.

He offered to carry some of it for me. "You can't get all this down the ladder in one trip."

Since the evening we had met, in Mary Lee's kitchen, our friendship had been easy and casually comfortable. He was clever, amusing, and he smelled clean. He was a playmate, someone I could laugh with. We stashed the provisions and then goofed around on the ladder for awhile, swaying it dangerously and swinging it sideways over the water. The game had a nostalgic flavor of childhood bike racing and hayloft climbs. The tomboy in me persisted.

We jumped onto the deck, swung down to the galley, and in a spirit of companionship and mutual agreement, laughingly unbuckled each other's jeans and got into a bunk.

Maybe this time, I thought, it will be different. But as always, there seemed to be some interference between my senses and my brain. I couldn't interpret this favorite of sports as either pleasant or unpleasant, just as I could never distinguish between boiling and freezing water. It was just meaningless horsing around. Something is wrong with me, I concluded, and probably always will be. Maybe it's the price I pay for lack of pain. I can prove to the world that I'm free and independent, but I'll never prove to myself that I'm not somehow abnormal.

It was impossible, however, to feel deprived of something that I had never experienced, never enjoyed. The deprivation was in the fact that this was just one more example of my insensitivity, one more to add to the list of human emotions and sensations I was cut off from. I could not conceive of loneliness or depression or physical pain. But psychological pain? Mental anguish? Injuries to the spirit and the soul? Oh, yes, I could find that kind of pain, if I looked. But I wouldn't.

There was no laughter as we left the boat and started back. Steen was unusually quiet and somber. *He knows now. He knows there's something wrong with me.* Too bad I couldn't have faked it, as I had learned to fake so many other things in order to appear normal.

I was introverted and melancholy as we looked for Bill at the Mayflower. He had already gone. I left Steen there and went home.

The phonograph played *I Pagliacci* and Bill sat on the couch, a half-finished gallon of Gallo wine at his feet.

"I got the lemons," I said, putting them in the ice box. The drip pan had begun to overflow again and I decided just to let it continue undisturbed. "And the squeezer," I added.

"You were gone so long," Bill said. "What did you do?"

"I ran into Steen and we went down to the boat. He helped me carry the stuff."

"You went down to the boat... with Steen?" He looked puzzled, incredulous, and anything but pleased.

"Yes."

"What did you *do?*" Alarm and rage were evident in his expression. I answered cautiously. Somehow, as if he'd scented it, I had the intuition that he already knew.

"I... we... nothing!"

He was on his feet in an instant, gripping my shoulders with an urgency and fury I had never seen before.

"*Don't... lie... to me!*"

"Bill, what is all this? Why should you care if I was with Steen? We've discussed all this. I don't ask you what you're doing!"

"You *screwed* him... *didn't* you!"

"Is that what you meant by 'soiling' our relationship?"

"*Didn't you!*" he demanded, eyes of fire staring into mine.

"Yes! Yes! I did! What does it matter?"

He sank back to the couch as though beaten.

"What matters is that you would lie to me," he said softly. "That's what would soil it. I can't stand to be lied to... by you of all people. If we don't have that, that honesty... we don't have anything."

"I understand that, Bill—I can't stand to be lied to either. But you were angry already! Why were you angry before I lied?"

"You think it's jealousy, don't you?" The laughter of Pagliacci rose incongruously in the background.

"I wouldn't recognize jealousy if I fell over it. I want to know why you were angry. You gave me a reason to lie. What reason would I have had to conceal what I did otherwise?"

"You certainly have a point there," Bill conceded. "Come sit down, sweetie."

I sat beside him, tucking my feet under me.

"Why?" I insisted. "Why were you angry?"

"It wasn't anger," he said sadly. "It was disillusionment. Disappointment at your behaving like a tramp. When I first saw you in the Mayflower, I saw such innocence... directness... incorruptibility."

"*You* inspired the directness. When I saw you I said, 'this is where I stop playing games. Here's someone who will see through them anyway. Someone who can accept me as I am.' Because that's what you were doing when you looked at me. Accepting me."

"But then you do a thing like this, sweetie. Cheapen my dream. Show me that it was an illusion. I saw you as chaste, pure, and I wanted to take you home just for the pleasure of your proximity. Just to be close to one good thing that was left in the world."

"But that's unfair, Bill!" I pounded the back of the couch with my fist. "It's unfair of you to attribute those qualities to me and then be disappointed in me when you find you're wrong. Besides, you knew yesterday that I was no virgin."

"You're right. Absolutely right, sweetie. But you still seemed to be virgin in your soul. It's as though you were my little sister, and I want the very best for you. And it would be best for you to abstain."

"But the fact of the matter is that if I abstain, and I usually do, it has nothing to do with virtue or strength of character. It's not will power or even the fear of Hell. So if I were a virgin you couldn't commend me for not doing something I had no desire to do! It's never been goodness in my case. It's deadness, Bill. Deadness! I'm not even alive sensually. All my nerves are dead."

"Then why?" he asked, obviously confounded. "Why did you... ?"

"It was an attempt at normalcy!" I blurted out.

"Normalcy!" Bill exclaimed. "Good Lord! Couldn't you think of a better place to start?"

* * *

After dinner, Bill tipped up the bottle to drain the last ounce.

"I've got to get to the package store before it closes. Want to walk with me?"

"I think I'll just take a bath and go to bed."

"It'll be a long time before I'll sleep," he said. "If I don't get back tonight, I'll see you on the boat."

I amended my decision, wanting to clear up a few things before morning. "I'll walk with you partway," I told him.

The sky had turned lavender with streaks of amber and orange, and we stopped in the road to watch its changes.

"If that were a painting, no one would believe it," I said.

"Mmm," Bill agreed. "It's got its own kind of beauty, but somehow I like sunrises better. Beginnings are better than endings."

He was strangely morose, and I thought of yesterday's conversation about Cliff.

"Bill, remember when you asked if I could walk away from you because of something I didn't understand?"

"And you said you couldn't."

"Could you?" I asked. "Could you walk away from me for that reason?"

"No, of course not. I'd try harder to understand."

"Well, yesterday when you suggested I imagine myself in Cliff's position, I knew I'd never be able to unless I could find out what was so great about sex."

"Oh, sweetie. There's nothing great about it at all."

"Then why is everybody looking for it?"

"Why does every drunk need a drink? It's a habit. It's as simple as that."

"Are you sure?"

"Of course I'm sure. You have a drink now and then, right? Do you have to become an alcoholic to understand why I need a drink?"

"But I enjoy a glass of wine."

"You'd enjoy a glass of grape juice just as much. You're a social drinker. God forbid that you should become a social screwer. There are enough of them around. Don't cultivate that awful habit."

"But it's not normal to have no desire at all! I'd like to have children someday, but how can I ever marry?"

"Ah, sweetie, what you see all around you is lust. What was it you said about the sunrise that first morning? 'Like singing hymns of praise. A bigger love, not a small personal love.' That's the way it can be for you."

"How do you know that such a thing is possible?"

"Because it was like that for me once. But it never will be again. Now I'm jaded and I do things to satisfy my lust… that would really put your understanding to a test, if you knew. But it doesn't have to be that way for you. It's not too late. You'll marry and you'll have your children, if you'll just put the whole thing out of your mind till then."

I had walked him all the way to the package store, and now we turned to go back.

"What about Steen?" I asked him. "I feel so strange about the whole thing. Now he's going to wonder what's wrong with me, and maybe he'll think there's something peculiar about you for putting up with me."

Bill laughed. "Steen *knows* there's something peculiar about me. Don't worry about it. I'll talk to Steen."

I didn't feel like going to bed now. I stayed downstairs with Bill after my bath and dozed off and on while he drank and we listened to Gregorian chants. In my half sleep and half stupor, we shared fantasies and dreams and fears like children alone in the dark.

By morning a small river had trickled into the room. We could look forward to another lake in a few days.

Chapter Six

At the end of the summer, when my mother and brother came to Provincetown to take me home to Albany County, Bill ran along beside the car, calling "151 West 21st Street! 151 West 21st Street! Don't forget!"

I stayed home just long enough to unpack my bags. After two weeks of wrangling with my mother, I packed them up again for the move to New York. Friends of hers had called ahead and arranged for me to share an apartment with another girl on West 86th Street, across from the side entrance to the Tip Toe Inn.

But as soon as I arrived in the city, I began to spend most of my free time in Bill's loft. We began by repainting the walls oyster white. He complained, "These people knew nothing about light, sweetie. Nothing whatever."

Far past the safe hours of night, when we weren't fixing the loft or sitting in the San Remo Cafe, Bill and I would traverse the city, dressed identically in pea coats and knit watch caps. We told each other we were conducting a longitudinal voyeuristic study. Our research method consisted of climbing fire escapes to look through the windows of people who thought they were alone.

Through the winter we kept notebooks of our findings, even

giving our subjects names to aid in discussion of what we had observed. Mr. DiCelza and his young blond secretary Brigitte danced the waltz to scratchy 78-rpm phonograph records. Ben Bruckster pored over want ads spread out on a table, his shoulders hunched in pain. Annie P. reached under her skirt and fingered herself, sprawled back, legs spread, in a big wooden rocking chair.

One night, watching breathlessly at a third-story window while a couple engaged in a raucous argument over housework, two men yelled at us from the street. "Hey! Get down from there!" And at the sound, the husband and wife inside looked right at us.

Bill, never one to follow instructions, grabbed my hand and yanked, tugging me up the fire escape to the roof. We jumped across to the next building, then down into an alley, where we huddled next to some garbage cans. I pulled my knit cap down tight and turned my skinny frame to the dirty brick wall. The two men who'd yelled at us walked by the alley entrance and peered in. "They there?" one asked.

"Just a couple of bums," the other said, and they walked on.

* * *

Neither Bill nor I did anything to contradict the widespread assumption that we were lovers. We each had something to gain in letting it stand. For me, the impression meant I wasn't forced to field passes or make excuses, and I was free to enjoy all the ironic freedom that "attachment" to a man conveyed.

Bill, on the other hand, must have liked the appearance that he was involved in a "normal," heterosexual, romantic relationship. He loved the drama and storminess of Cathy and Heathcliff. All the same, even in public and despite the depraved window-peeping, he always acted as a big brother to me. He urged me to behave myself, to abstain from sex until I was married, so often that it became tiresome. He pointed out his own mistakes as pitfalls to be avoided, holding himself up or down as an example not to be followed.

Bill felt completely at home on the rooftops of Manhattan. One afternoon we went to a movie full of Arabs leaping off buildings and shooting at each other from behind doors and things. When we got back to the loft, we immediately wrapped sheets around ourselves, grabbed water pistols and ran out into the street. Allen Ginsberg, walking by the street entrance lost in thought, stopped and stared at us, open-mouthed, as we ran by.

I chased Bill onto the roof before I realized how foolish that was when he'd been drinking. Suddenly uneasy, I stopped, refusing to follow him as he jumped from building to building.

There was a blanket on the roof for sunbathing and I sat on it, arranging my sheet to take advantage of the sun. Bill returned in a roundabout way, sneaking up behind me. He got me with a blast of cold water right between the shoulder blades, and I fell over, playing dead. He sat down beside me and said, "You know what we need up here?"

"A pool!" I answered without hesitation.

"Well, okay, but I was thinking of a bar."

"You'd have half the city up here."

"The more the merrier! Maybe I'd get you and Kerouac together then. I've been wanting to play matchmaker but you never show up at the same time."

"Matchmaker!" I laughed. "I much prefer being an observer, not a participant in the affairs of the heart."

"One of these days, you'll find yourself entangled," Bill warned me. "I just hope your libido isn't awakened until you are married, sweetie. I hope you wait for marriage for that. I don't want you to turn out like me."

I rolled my eyes, and for a few moments we were silent. I felt steam rising from the back of my wet shirt. Finally my curiosity got the better of me, and I asked "Why Kerouac, anyway? What's his first name?"

"Jack. He's a drunk. Not as bad as I am but a drunk nevertheless. He likes to hang around and be entertained by me. I hung by my feet from the fire escape for him."

"Bill, you are the perpetual Pagliacci," I told him. "What's this Kerouac do?"

"He's a writer, and *mensch* in his own way. He takes care of his mother. Has some middle class ideas about marriage and he's very serious about settling down and having a family."

"And you want to introduce him to *me*?" I laughed incredulously.

***

Bill had circle upon circle of friends, like an endless series of rings. They ran the gamut from artists and educators to bums and hustlers. Some were former Harvard classmates, concerned about Bill's progressive alcoholism and his neglect of a potentially brilliant legal career. Others, like Jack Kerouac, were new acquaintances, more familiar with Bill's bizarre drunken behavior than with his incredible mind. I suspected that, for the newer crowd, Bill was of more value as a novelty, a conversation piece. I'd overhear them discussing his flirtations with death as if it were all some zany game for their benefit.

I delightedly let myself be drawn into his lunatic activities, all the same. Once we played football in the snow outside the Bleeker Street Tavern. A particularly enthusiastic tackle brought me down on a buried hydrant, and I broke a tooth.

"It doesn't hurt, don't worry," I told Bill. "I can't feel pain."
And it was true, I didn't feel a thing.

Another time we were walking on Fulton Street where a construction crew was drilling concrete. Bill suddenly began singing
I Pagliacci at the top of his lungs. I joined in, trying to stifle my
outbursts of laughter.

The crew stopped drilling, mystified, and when we finished
they good-naturedly applauded us.

At other times, the bare intensity of being Bill's friend made
me shiver with emotion. Just before Christmas, we stood hand in
hand in the Fifth Avenue Presbyterian Church, listening to
Handel's *Messiah*, and the solemn commitment we felt toward
each other flooded my soul. Bill was my companion, confidant,
buddy and playmate, commiserator and confirmer, affirmer,
counselor and advisor, but never my judge, critic, or reformer.

And he was so outlandish and careless with his life that as
often as he reminded me, I reminded myself: I mustn't need him,
mustn't care.

* * *

In February of 1950, I was job hunting. My mother had
insisted that I needed to work to be able to stay in the city, and in
my eagerness, I followed up all leads and hunches. Waiting for an
afternoon appointment on 71st Street, I stopped at a coffee shop
on West End Avenue. I mentioned to the waiter that I was looking for a job, and asked if he knew of anything in the neighborhood. He said something about a painter down the block who was
looking for a receptionist with an art background.

I went immediately to ring his doorbell. His name was Pio
Junco, a small Cuban man. Pio brought me into the studio and
introduced me off-handedly to the student who rented a room in

the seven-room apartment.

The tenant's name was Herb Lashinsky, and he was slightly overweight and very aloof. He hardly acknowledged our intro- duction, and went to his room shortly. Pio told me he could not use a full-time receptionist, but he had a friend, a fellow painter, who also needed help. Perhaps I could combine the two part-time jobs. I agreed to give it a try.

* * *

Within a week, some spark ignited into open passion between Herb and me. I found myself running up the four flights of stairs to the loft. "Bill!" I yelled breathlessly as I flung open the door. "It's a miracle!"

"Sweetie?" Bill asked, alarmed.

"I've been transformed from observer to participant!"

On and on I went about Herb Lashinsky, young physicist doing graduate work at Columbia, explaining sophomorically that this man was the exception to all my rules. My barriers were coming down, and I found I was a woman after all.

Bill listened gravely. When I finally wound to a stop, he looked at me with sadness and concern. "Sweetie, you know you stand to be left with nothing but wounds and disillusionment," he said.

I tried to entice him to share my enthusiasm. "Bill!" I said. "It's just what you wanted for me! Singing hymns of praise? Watching the sunrise? Remember?"

But Bill just gazed at me unhappily. "This lover," he said dis- tastefully. "He seems to have... awakened your libido. And you know what, sweetie? I had hoped you'd wait for marriage for that."

"Oh, Bill," I answered. "Surely you know it's better to feel... something, than the nothing, the painless bubble of nothing, that I have been living up to now."

"The longer you stay with him," Bill predicted, "the greater your need will be."

"So you're going to tell me I should throw away my vision, my vision of real love? I'd have to, you know. Because the vision and Herb are interwoven now. They're inextricable."

"No, no," Bill said gently. "It's like anything else. You just have to pare it down to a realizable, manageable size."

"I'd abandon it before I'd do that," I insisted.

"Bring him to the loft, sweetie," Bill said gently. "You know your big brother has to meet him."

***

I brought Herb to the loft, telling myself it wasn't so much for approval, but because I wanted to share him. I wanted these two loves of mine to see each other's beauty. Still, I was unable to shake the intuition that it would be a disaster. And as it turned out, things went far worse than I would have believed they could.

While I tried desperately to steer the conversation toward music or literature, where they might have had something in common, Bill launched an attack on quantum mechanics. Astounding me with a skill beyond his law school prerogative, he quoted from Plato, Spinoza, and Einstein, arguing the limitations of conventional forms of measurement.

Herb grew more and more red in the face. He might have listened to such an approach from a colleague, someone well grounded in physics. But from a renegade lawyer who didn't even go to work, made no attempt to dress decently, and was a drunk to boot, this audacious brilliance was unforgivable.

Bill had hit below the belt. And Herb countered, throwing Plato back at Bill, molding an equally devastating discourse on social conscience and responsibility, accusing Bill of deserting his colors.

As we said our strained good nights, I could almost see Bill's and my voyeuristic notebooks about to be moved into storage, tucked away in some recess of the loft.

* * *

Herb and I found an apartment at 13 Charlton Street, and all that had been mundane became extraordinary in our double perspective. We had been shaped by totally dissimilar frameworks of circumstance and experience. Even our learning and problem-solving methods were different. In the first bloom of wonder and excitement over this dynamic interaction of opposites, we rediscovered together the places, arts, and ideas we had come to love alone. We viewed everything new through each other's eyes. But I was consumed with giddiness, indulging myself in all the adolescent fantasies I had sidestepped at their proper time, suffering the kind of pulse-wrenching crush that should only victimize teenage girls. I firmly believed that there could be no other for me.

Neither of us could cope with the plague of emotional ups and downs that now visited me. I must have appeared childish and more than a little crazy to Herb, although I believed that after years of living in a bubble, insulated and booby-trapped for self-protection, I was finally opening up and becoming healthy, becoming normal.

Herb found it impossible to take me seriously, and I couldn't tell him what I was going through. Afraid of stumbling verbally and further reducing my credibility in his eyes, I suffered from a sort of intellectual impotence. My inability and, truthfully, my disinclination to come up to his standards of educational achievement and professional worth made me doubt his acceptance of me, though he did nothing to either confirm or allay my suspicions.

It took only weeks before my doubts became crippling. I saw

that we were unable to communicate our feelings to each other at all, and I was unable to believe that Herb cared about me in any but a casual way. One afternoon, I worked myself into a frenzy.

Hurling my clothes and belongings frantically into my bags, I rushed out of the apartment, and begged my friend Sarah to let me move in. Foolishly, I told myself that if Herb wanted me back, he'd say so.

He had too much pride for that. He moved out, too.

Co-owners now of a treasure of broken rules, broken dreams and shattered visions, Herb and I continued to see each other. But nothing brought us closer to resolution. And for me the agony was worse each time I saw him.

I perversely reacted by becoming all the things he couldn't accept. We had never been each other's ideal in the first place. When he was his usual, self-possessed self, Herb had never been in the least attractive to me. As the confident, well-dressed grad student, I had no use for him. Sometimes when I watched him talk to his colleagues, I felt only cold indifference toward him.

It was because of what I had seen at those unguarded times, stolen as it were, that I loved him. I kept those moments as part of myself for safe-keeping.

***

Late in October, as Herb and I sat unhappily gazing at each other over rum babka in the San Remo Cafe, Bob Steen came to our table.

"Bill's been killed," he said, his face contorted with grief.

"*What!?*" I cried out.

"It was a subway accident. Oh, Joan, he tried to climb out the window of a moving train."

I sat, unmoving, stunned to the depth of my heart. "Then he

finally killed himself," I said stupidly.

I rose without thinking, left Herb sitting there and ran down the street, passing green news stands without stopping for the confirmation they offered. I rushed to my room and secluded myself there, locked myself in, turned my mind inward, grieving. I stayed in the room after that for days—I don't even know how long I stayed there. I thought maybe I'd never come out.

Bill! You left me without forgiving me for letting my libido be awakened. Oh, Bill! I'll put it back to sleep again, I promise.

* * *

Herb visited me twice, but I didn't leave the room until Bill's brother Fred came down from Croton-on-the-Hudson to knock at my door.

I opened the door to an apparition. It was Bill, only healed, healthy and vigorous. The same wiry frame, olive skin and soulful brown eyes. The same small mouth with full lips. The loose curls of his dark hair. But, miraculously, no alcoholic pallor, no circles around the eyes, no wine-stains on the lips.

"Joan?" he asked. "I'm—"

"Yes," I stopped him. "I know who you are, but just stand there like that for a minute and... be Bill."

We clung together then in a hug of mutual deprivation.

"I want you to help me sort out Bill's things," Fred said. "I could really use your help packing and organizing."

We went to the loft with boxes, and began the dreary work of packing papers, pictures, clothing, books and records. When we came to the sole painting on the wall, Cezanne's *Mardi Gras*, I stopped and stared at it. I had always thought it was in the wrong place, somehow. Not above the bed, as you'd expect, but on the adjacent expanse of bare wall. It was as if it waited for a specific piece of furniture to be set beneath it.

"Was that Bill's?" Fred asked.

"Yes."

"Do you want it?"

"No. I wish it could stay here." I sighed. "What's going to happen to this place now?"

"I imagine they'll rent it as soon as possible."

"I hate to think of anyone changing things. Painting these walls. Bill loved the light in this place."

Fred considered me. Finally he asked, "Do you want to rent it? I could arrange it."

I thought about it. If I did, everything could stay the same. It seemed a good enough reason. "Why not?" I agreed.

We went to the realtor, who said wearily that he had to know I would use it for professional purposes only. I was a designer-dressmaker, I said. That filled the bill. Papers were signed, and a few days later, I moved in.

Chapter Seven

Herb came to pick me up at my new apartment, just a few days later. It was evening by the time he arrived. We started downtown. An erratic breeze had come up, swirling dirty bits of debris around our feet, threatening our eyes with cinders. My legs were as long as Herb's, and our steps were in unison, but our thoughts were not.

I had probably envisioned dinner at The Fireside as a vehicle for reconciliation. Herb and I had seen each other only infrequently since the afternoon I'd slammed out of the apartment in my frenzy of doubt. Herb's icy response that day had left us both feeling wounded and lost, so we came together from time to time, like amputees seeking a lost limb. And in proximity, the wounds refused to heal.

We entered the restaurant with a serious and decorous air, polished for the occasion. Herb's tweed sport coat was appropriate for a graduate student on the town. My own careful attire was ambiguous; a billowing skirt, disguising my thinness, and a blue-green silk shirt. I had brushed my dark hair till it gleamed. Herb took my coat with gentlemanly aplomb. We were shown to our table and took our places facing each other across the white expanse. We had all the courtesy and restraint of a couple on their first date. The waiter brought rolls and butter, poured ice from a clinking pitcher, placed menus before us and left us to our own devices.

"Your shirt matches your eyes. Very attractive." Herb's voice flowed over me like warm water. I nodded and considered his own eyes, his brown, gentle, luminous eyes, but decided this might not be the best possible topic of conversation.

"How was your week?" I ventured.

"Just fine. How was yours?"

"It was swell."

He winced. "Can't you find a better adjective than that?"

"What's wrong with 'swell?' It's just another word, like great, fine, nice...dandy."

"You can express yourself without using slang. 'Swell' makes you sound like a country girl, uneducated."

"You're right. It was a bad choice," I said coldly. "Actually my week was lousy, now that I think about it. Just lousy!"

He sighed like an exasperated parent. The sound stirred a pleasant nostalgia for me, taking me home to our apartment where I had habitually tried his patience.

He broke a roll, buttered both halves, and handed one across to me, asking "Hmmm?"

I put out my hand for it, frowning a little at him. I hated the inference as I accepted it that I was a child, incapable of deciding whether I needed a roll, and incompetent to butter it. His gesture offered me symbolism: a roll to remind us of our familiar roles.

His own menu open, he tapped mine twice with his finger. I ignored the menu and looked at the back of his hand. I was tempted to count each black hair as if to make sure they were all still there.

"See what you want to eat," he said, bending to his menu with the same attitude of concentration I remembered watching from our bed, half dozing, while he studied at his desk across the room. Late at night I had listened for the reassuring sound of his bare feet on the wood floor, heels hitting solidly, the steps of a man who knew what he was about.

I opened my menu quickly and searched for something to answer the next question. *What will be sacrificed tonight in honor of our presence here, separated by white cloth and wood? Will it be cattle, swine, fish, or fowl?*

"What looks good to you?" he asked.

"What do you think?" I stalled.

"Filet of sole, I think." His eyes met mine briefly, as the waiter appeared to take our order.

I stared at the menu, flushing, unable to speak, consumed with the doubt that beset me: Was the whole of Herb and me greater than the sum of ourselves, or were we each reduced by our union. Herb and the waiter looked silently at me.

"The lady isn't ready," Herb finally told him.

My shoulders relaxed a bit as the waiter left. I had a second chance. I'd try again now to tell him what I should have told him in the beginning. I'd get out my secret guilts and treasures, put them right here on the table where he could either accept or reject them once and for all.

"Herb, I have to tell you something very important." My voice trembled.

I remembered a time when I had said those very words to him, and he had answered me, "Okay, tell me." But by now, he knew I could not fully speak my mind about us.

So he smiled and said "It's all right. You don't have to tell me."

"But I do!" I took a deep breath. The enormity of the risk welled up in my chest. Tears burned to get out, my throat constricted, my mouth went dry.

He watched me.

"I can't," I sighed at last. "I just can't."

"It's all right, Joan. I know. Just tell me what you want for dinner."

I stared at the table, wondering, *What does he know? What does he think he knows? Or does he even care?*

"All I want is a small tossed salad and a glass of milk."

"Joan, don't do that! Order sensibly, will you? Sometimes you embarrass me."

"But you don't know. You don't know my needs or my condition. You wouldn't want me to order a full meal just to please you."

"I wish that just once it would please *you* to do something properly."

"I guess it's become a matter of principle."

"Principle!" he cried in exasperation.

* * *

Once outside, we walked in stride and in strained silence, and I knew that we were writing the epitaph of our relationship tonight. I stepped across a small rock, resisting the urge to kick it ahead of me, remembering how often I'd done that as a girl. It had been a way of disguising with idle activity all the frenzy in my head.

I always saw any attempt to direct my energies or correct my opinions as a design to deprive me of my ability to think, and as a child, I'd answer any such attempt with silence and isolation. My grandfather was the only adult who could guide my thinking gently, helping me to learn the ways my own mind worked. Later, I learned to envision myself as a chameleon, developing tactics to stop being seen as an anti-social introvert; I'd move in and out of inane schoolyard conversations, contributing my own contrived inanities, uttering some irrelevancy when pressed for an opinion. When I was sixteen I was convinced I was certifiably insane, that I could never fit in with the world, that I was hopelessly set against it. But this conviction didn't frighten me. It delighted me.

I glanced sidelong at Herb. I'd tried not to disguise myself with him, to let my opinions find honest voice, to show my beliefs without fear. He met my views with his trained scientific mind, demanding documentation, sources, authority. How could I tell him that my source was a spider, and that each of us has, in every cell, an allotment of that knowledge? Could I somehow find a way to introduce Herb to the spirit of my grandfather?

One day I had said to him, "Science is trying to explain God."

"That's nothing new," he had answered. "Isaac Newton said that more than 200 years ago."

"Well, but I didn't know that. Are you accusing me of plagiarism?"

"Of course not. Look at who Newton was. When he said it, it meant something."

"Then when I say it, it means nothing? I worked to come to that conclusion too, you know. Does my statement lack validity because I have no reputation? Is that it?"

"It's unnecessary, that's all! If you had an education, you'd know what's already been said and what's already been done. You could save yourself all this trouble of thinking if you'd go to school! "

"That wouldn't be the same!" I had objected. "Just knowing that Newton had said it wouldn't tell me what he meant by it. You can't know something like that without experiencing it!"

"Newton knew it," Herb answered. "He experienced it for the rest of posterity."

***

Now Herb broke the silence as we walked. "What are you thinking about?"

"Incest," I said truthfully.

"What?"

"Do you know why incest is condemned?" I asked him. "Other than the moral issue, I mean."

"You tell me." He shook his head in consternation.

"Because the offspring could be deficient or defective! Right?" I looked at him. "Unhealthy recessive genes could result in progeny without vigor. Hemophilia, for instance. I think..." I paused, flustered, not sure about hemophilia, anxious not to lose the thought before I got it out.

"Why don't you go to school and become a biologist?" he asked, throwing me off.

"Don't!" I stamped my foot. "You make me forget what I'm saying."

"Okay. What are you saying?" he prompted.

"Just follow me a minute. Trust me."

"Trust *you*?"

I ignored this, trying again. "What would be the product of a union of very similar thinking processes?"

"A defective or deficient idea?" he offered.

"Yes! I think so. Maybe a stagnant idea. Nothing more than mutual confirmation. At best."

"All right, go on."

"Herb, the product of dissimilar thinking processes would be healthier! There would be a greater chance of something new developing."

"Doesn't that depend upon how dissimilar they are?" he asked. "What if they're too dissimilar to even get their ideas together in the first place?"

I stopped cold. It was obviously his analysis of our predicament. And where could you go from there?

* * *

I had once brought an article to high school, a summary of the discovery of how bacteria mutate from one strain to another, a finding that would lead to the discovery of DNA. I showed it to my teacher. The things we had been learning in school about heredity and immunity flew in the face of the facts outlined in this article. But he merely glanced at it before dismissing it as "interesting but irrelevant."

I felt anger and frustration following this dismissal, emotions that turned inward and began to take a physical toll. Pains in my stomach and head destroyed my appetite, and I went to bed with a fever. I thought the agony of my silent pain and rage would surely consume me, and then, in an instant, a startling change occurred. It was as if I had been pushed through a sheet of glass, but the glass didn't break, and now I was intact behind it. All feeling was mercifully shut off, the world was closed out, and I learned to float on a cloud of detachment. And that cloud sustained me for years.

But Herb had brought spring, started my sap flowing, made detachment impossible. I had been self-centered; now my center expanded to include him. I felt electric with potential when I was with him. His organization and discernment were qualities I lacked. I responded to his intellect, longing to mingle with it, but not willing to do that without his approval. I had prevented seduction of my own mind. I would not now violate his.

I knew my ideas were ingrown and inbred from feeding on themselves. I longed for him to stir his ideas in, to make mine spark and grow, to help me learn. But I couldn't speak to him in the scientific terms he demanded, the language he understood. I knew only the language of metaphor and analogy, which he refused to hear . And that barrier prevented us from communicating, right up to tonight, as we walked silently along a dark New York street.

* * *

I remembered one Saturday morning, sweeping the apartment, when I had begun sifting through the dustpan to retrieve a small bead, a straight pin, and a button. Suddenly I was conscious of Herb watching me, his face full of incomprehension.

"What are you doing?" he asked.

"It would be wasteful to throw these things away," I said defensively.

"But it's a waste of time to do that. You get sidetracked from everything you do. How do you expect to ever get anything done that way, daydreaming, contemplating irrelevancies?"

"There's nothing that's irrelevant," I answered stubbornly. "Nothing."

"Irrelevant to the task at hand."

"But what is the task at hand? What is it really? Nothing is too big or too small. I know you think I should follow some direct path and get some single thing done. But there is no single thing in this world I would choose to do over all other single things. Unless, unless it would be an idea."

"What would you *do* with an idea?"

"I'd do nothing with it, I'd do everything with it! I'd *live* it. If I could explain that to you, there would be no need to explain anything else, ever."

"Try. Try, then."

I didn't answer. I could only think, *when we're very old and it will be of some value to you. Then I'll wrap it in a cobweb, hung with dewdrops. It will be my gift to you. Because it will be the only thing I have to give.*

A bead in the dustpan, a star in the cosmos. What do I sweep? Dust, irrelevancies, metaphors?

***

Glancing at Herb again, flushed with frustration, I suddenly felt a sense of loss that was overwhelming. The loss was most painful because it was of potential, of something never had, of something only hoped for. I looked for something to focus my attention on, something to simply confirm my existence, right here, right now, on Seventh Avenue, on November 3rd, 1950. And suddenly I spied another small rock, and this time I fell out of step and began to kick it, keeping it just ahead of me.

Intent on my own thoughts, now, wondering if rocks had any kind of awareness of their own, I helped this little rock turn the corner onto 21st Street, and I almost collided with an old man who scuffled along, bent low by the weight of his shopping bag.

Herb pulled me roughly out of the way. "Watch where you're going!" he admonished me. "Can't you stop being such a child?"

I ducked away from him to retrieve my rock and kick it back into line. Determined not to appear acquiescent, I continued to kick it long after losing interest, all the way to my building. At the door, I stopped to look around at my new neighborhood.

Two cultures occupied this space, one superimposed on the other. The nightly transformation had begun in our absence. The hum of machines in manufacturing lofts had ceased, lights had been turned off, the factory workers had stampeded down wooden stairs onto the street in the rush for a subway seat home. For some interval, the street was empty, dark, and quiet. Then lights began to appear in top floor windows, as clandestine loft dwellers came to life, turned up their music and revealed their existence to the night.

I looked up at the loft that I had visited so many times when it belonged to Bill. Now it was mine, and the windows were dark. Lucien Carr's were bright, in line with mine on the top floor of the adjoining building. There appeared to be a party going on at Lu's. Music poured down from there as forms crossed and recrossed the windows.

Herb waited for me at the entrance door to 151 West 21st Street. I sensed his impatience, but I stopped to pick up the rock and drop it into my trench coat pocket before going up to meet him.

"What about rocks?" I asked, unlocking the huge black entrance door and then closing it to be sure it locked once we were inside. "Do you suppose they have any kind of awareness or consciousness?"

"Not the rocks in your head!" Playfully, chidingly, he grabbed the back of my neck. I knew his signals, and ordinarily I would have turned toward him. But tonight I accepted some inevitability, and I turned away, and we started the long climb up the four flights of stairs.

Chapter Eight

We were at Bill Cannastra's door. No, it had become my door. I unlocked it and reached inside for the light switch. Herb just dropped into a chair and picked up a magazine. I hung the keys on their nail by the front window and clopped across the bare wood floor to the kitchen, throwing my coat over a storage cabinet on the way. Not sure what I was up to, I pulled pots and pans out of the cupboard, carefully and certainly dropping them on the floor to make as much racket as possible.

How could he sit there and read? Didn't he know we weren't going to see each other again? Didn't we have anything to settle finally... some last-minute explanations or clarifications? Some good wishes for each other at least?

The noise had the desired effect.

"Now you're hungry?" he asked. "Couldn't you have eaten at the restaurant?"

"I ate!"

"A bunch of leaves!"

"A salad was all I wanted, Herb," I said, too quietly.

"What are you cooking?"

I had no idea. I took some baker's cocoa down from the shelf and distractedly shook it into a sauce pan.

A shout came up from the street.

"Helloooooooo!"

"Would you look out and see who that is?" I asked, pretending to be busy.

"You look. It's your window."

I threw the spoon into the pan and made the trek to the front window, commenting as I passed, "Sure! It's only half a block from one end of this place to the other."

I opened the window and looked down, shouting "Who is it?"

"Kerouac!"

I stood there only a fraction of a moment before yelling, "I'll throw you the keys. Come on up!"

My aim wasn't good but he easily covered the distance to catch them. Herb asked, "Who's that, and why are you letting him up?"

"Friend of Lucien Carr's and Allen Ginsberg's... and Bill's. Bill spoke of him."

"What did he say about him?"

But Jack Kerouac was with us already, having run up the stairs. A neatly pressed young man with carefully combed dark hair and very blue eyes, he had the appearance of being well cared-for, as though he belonged to somebody. His features were just coarse enough to keep him from being pretty. Setting an attache case by the door, he entered the room and offered the keys to Herb, who gestured in my direction.

"Oh! It's your place?"

I nodded. "I'm Joan. This is Herb."

"Jack!" he said, shaking Herb's hand. "Somebody told me there was a party here tonight."

"Probably at Lucien's," I told him. "But we can have a hot chocolate party. I was just making some."

I left to go back to the kitchen and heard Jack ask Herb, "Your girl?"

"Nope," was Herb's answer. I stopped in mid-step, out of their sight, stung. He might as well have said, "She's fair game."

It seemed to me as I poured the chocolate that Herb could have come up with a more ambiguous answer, understanding the spirit of Jack's question. But I was determined to accept that this was how Herb wanted it, and resigned that this was how I wanted it, too.

Jack was still standing and Herb was still sitting when I returned with the tray and set it down on a small table. Two folding chairs leaned against the wall and I went to get them. Jack immediately, chivalrously, rushed to take them from me.

"What do you do, Jack?" Herb asked.

"Oh, well, I. . ." He spread his hands as though whatever he did wasn't of much importance. "I wrote a book." He looked down at his feet and then up again, grinning slightly, almost bashfully. "I'm writing another one," he added, sitting down.

"What about?"

"Well, this one's about my travels. All over the country. And Mexico too!"

"Sounds interesting," Herb remarked unconvincingly, and went back to his magazine.

Jack burned his mouth on his drink. "Wow, this is hot!"

"I'm sorry," I said. "I should have told you."

Herb raised his eyebrows over the magazine. I suddenly realized that I must have sounded sarcastic. I hadn't meant to. I was being misunderstood at every step this evening. I wanted Jack to know that I wasn't trying to belittle him.

"Would you like some cold milk in it?" I asked, to make amends.

"No, no. That's all right. It'll cool. You live here all alone?"

I nodded.

"Did you know Bill very well?"

"Yes," I said tersely, backing off instantly. "But tell me about your first book. Was that about traveling too?"

"No, it was about a big family. In a small town." He went to get his attache case and removed a book from it. I saw at least five more copies inside before he closed the case and set it on the floor.

"Here." He handed me the book. "This is for you."

I read the title aloud. "*The Town and the City*." I turned it over to look at his picture on the back. Photo by Arni.

"It doesn't look like you," I commented.

"Nah! Guy was a faggot. Made me look like one, too. Next time I'm going to have my picture taken with my hair all messed up and a big old plaid lumberjack shirt on."

Herb looked up from his magazine to ask, "The real you?"

"Yeah, I guess you could say so," Jack answered defensively.

I shot a censoring look at Herb. I felt protective. Jack was... harmless. He didn't deserve ridicule. Opening the book, I said, "You'll have to autograph it for me."

He obliged immediately, taking a pen from his pocket and signing the bottom of the flyleaf. Then, way up at the top he wrote "For Joan," saying, "When I know you better I'll add something to that."

He set the book on the table and finished his chocolate. Herb put down his magazine and picked up the book.

"Thanks," I said. "I'll start reading it tonight."

"No, don't do that. I've got a better idea. Let's all go over to Lucien's party."

"We weren't invited," Herb said.

"I'm inviting you. That's good enough. Whadaya say?"

I nodded encouragement to Herb and he compromised, "Well, maybe for a little while."

"Hey! We don't even have to go downstairs!" Jack exclaimed. "We can go right across the fire escape."

"Can we do that?" Herb asked me.

"Sure. We'll just go out my kitchen window and into Lu's. Allen comes over that way all the time to use my shower."

"You'd better put on a pair of jeans if you're going to climb around on fire escapes," Herb suggested.

"Aw, you look nice in your dress," Jack objected.

I considered, then put on my coat and carried the tray to the kitchen. Herb followed me, saying quietly, wearily, "Put on your jeans."

"There's nobody down there!" I was defiant, but I tried to give it a teasing tone. Herb sighed and looked away.

I asked him, in a softer tone, before Jack came into the kitchen, "Why did you have to answer that way when he asked if I was your girl?"

"It's your show. You're the one who left. Aren't you a big girl now?"

I blinked, and then I stepped out onto the fire escape, turning to see if Jack was watching. He followed with his attache case, a silly grin on his face. Herb brought up the rear. Just a few feet later we were entering Lu's kitchen.

"Well! Will you look who's here!" Lucien greeted us. "You do make some grand entrances, Jack, old boy! Hi Joan, and uh, Herb, isn't it?"

This was not Herb's favorite group of people. He suffered them through association with me, and I had become associated with them through Bill.

Introductions were made and drinks poured all around. Herb took his to the front window and stood beside the phonograph, looking down at the darkness below, while Billie Holiday sang "Lover Man" to street and loft alike. Jack made a place for me on the sofa by removing several record albums. He was clearly the *cause celebre*, and a crowd surrounded us immediately. Leaning back comfortably against a huge yellow cushion, Jack held court.

Lu's girl, Liz, rushed back and forth effervescently. Seeing Jack, she stopped and exclaimed huskily, "Oh Jack! Lovey!" She kissed him wildly.

"And Cathy!" She kissed me too. "I didn't know you knew each other."

"Cathy?" Jack asked me.

"No, it's Joan. It's a long story, Jack. Ask me again... someday."

Liz's hair, a new shade of strawberry blond, bounced as the rest of her did. She had an appealing compact roundness and was always in motion, forever exuberant. I enjoyed being with her, admired her lack of restraint, though I was sometimes embarrassed by her loudness on the subway when she singled out an ad or poster for her favorite indictment: "My *Gawd*! Did you ever see *any*thing so re*ac*tionary?"

Lu said she reminded him of a puppy, and it was easy to see why. I had never known anyone with a friendlier, more vivacious personality.

"You look like spring," I told her, referring to her pink and white checked calico dress.

"Yes! And in November! I just felt like it was time. Everything's been so gloomy around here."

Allen Ginsberg, wringing thin nervous hands together like a fly, entered the court. He peered at me intently with dark somber eyes behind horn-rimmed glasses.

"Did I leave my soap at your place?" he asked seriously, almost whispering.

A pert blonde perched on the arm of the sofa and played with Jack's hair familiarly. "Where've you been keeping yourself, Jack?"

I answered Allen in a conspiratorial tone, "I think so. There's a foreign bar of soap in my shower."

"Oh, you know," Jack said to the blonde. "My mom... she gets lonely."

"Pink?" Allen asked.

"Uh-huh. Smells like cinnamon."

"Well, bring her with you," said the blonde. "I'd like to meet your mom."

"Yeah, that's it. Cinnamon," Allen confirmed.

"I'll take good care of it," I assured Allen, who nodded and then leaned across me to tell the blonde:

"His mom wouldn't like you. She doesn't like any of Jack's friends. On principle."

"Is that right, Jack?" she asked him.

"I dunno. I guess she seems that way sometimes."

The girl spied someone else she knew and was off.

"Who was that girl?" I asked Jack.

"I don't know! Must have been drunk, 'cause I sure don't remember meeting her." He laughed as though this were a huge joke on himself.

I looked to see who had attracted the blonde's attention. It was a girl who, weeks ago, had been contemplating an abortion. Judging by her slim figure, she had decided to go through with it. Liz now advised her stridently, "But you *can't* go on *flag*ellating yourself, you know!" I felt a strange tingling in my womb, and it almost made me dizzy.

Allen joined the trio to commiserate about the abortion, and John Holmes took the seat he had vacated. Easing his lanky frame onto the sofa, he abruptly re-opened what must have been a long-running conversation. "I see what you mean, Jack, about Celine's spontaneity," he said. "I've been reading him all week."

"Yeah! Wow! Isn't he great? He just gets going and never stops."

An older man I didn't know, who had come in with Holmes, interjected, "He's such a cynic though, and his attitude toward women is terrible. Like what he says about Musyne, 'Women are all housemaids at heart.'"

"Oh, well," Jack began, "he knows what women are, really, and what they're for."

"What are they for, Jack?" Holmes egged him on.

"Well, women. . ." He looked at me sheepishly. "They're children. Just big beautiful children, that's all."

I was charmed, despite myself, at how Jack got himself off the hook.

"They're inferior then? You agree with Celine?" the older man wanted to know.

"Nah! Not inferior! Are children inferior? They're beautiful. I love 'em."

Allen entered the discussion. "What does it matter what Celine thinks of women? How does he write? That's all that matters."

"Spontaneity, that's all," Jack said. "That's everything!"

***

I caught a glimpse of Bob Steen's yellow hair by the door where he spoke to some late arrivals. When he turned around, our eyes met in a brief greeting. His smile was peculiarly attractive, and I returned it, but inwardly I was recalling what he'd said to me several days after our afternoon in a bunk on the *Piraga* in Provincetown. "You like to hurt people, don't you?" he had accused me.

I hadn't understood what he meant, and still didn't tonight, and didn't know if I wanted to. Was it my lack of enthusiasm? The fact that the event wasn't repeated? Or was it something else having nothing to do with that afternoon? I had entered into the activity out of curiosity. It was just one more attempt to discover what all the furor was about. And one more failure.

Now in the light of my relationship with Herb, I saw how cold and unresponsive I had been in the past. I could walk away from lovers without caring whether or not I saw them again, and I assumed the indifference was mutual. My love for Herb had changed that. I now had some compassion, some understanding of the emotions and caring that could accompany a relationship.

Maybe someday I would ask Steen whether that was what he had meant by that remark. Tonight wasn't the time.

* * *

Jack became more captivating and more charming as night and drink progressed. He was reveling in each comment, every crazy antic, loving the life of his friends, now giggling at some absurdity, now voicing one of his own. Occasionally some dark gloom would halt the laughter, but it didn't last. The next moment had him chuckling into his cushion as if he had translated some remark into a private language and found an uncommonly funny *double entendre*. I found myself laughing at his laughter.

I caught Herb's eye across the room and, on the verge of exchanging eye messages, we looked away from each other, like cats checking themselves in mid-pounce. A sob began to rise inside me, replacing that fleeting moment of exhilaration. I had to get away from the noise.

"Excuse me," I said to Jack. "Be right back." I went to the back of the loft. There was no one in the kitchen, and I slipped out the fire escape window to sit on the cold iron grating and look at the city through the railing.

Looking over the sparkling lights in the night, my tired brain wandered off on its own course, and I found myself thinking of my grandfather and how spiders make webs. I smiled at the reverie, and then stopped, startled. I blinked, and looked again at the twinkling city, and now I saw again the view before me as I had seen it in my dream, my dream in my mother's house in Albany County, more than a year before.

Letting my gaze drift over the dark neighborhood, I half-closed my eyes, and the city lights were like the drops of dew that sparkled on that spider's web in the dawn, so many years before. I watched the fragile strands sway in the chill, and I murmured to the memory of my grandfather, "Who taught the people how to build this beautiful city?"

I had no answer for myself. But I found myself wondering something else now. What would happen to a spider if it was kept in a small box where it couldn't spin webs? Would it assume that it was meant never to make webs at all, and so never try again, even if it was released?

Or would it make up for lost time when it was released by crazily spinning web after web?

* * *

Someone was in the kitchen behind me, but I didn't turn around till the figure put a hand on my shoulder and I knew it wasn't Herb.

"'S matter?" Jack asked. "You okay?"

"Sure," I said, swinging my legs inside. "Just needed some air."

Herb met us as we came in from the kitchen. Things had gotten out of hand in the few minutes I'd been outside. A lamp had been smashed. Someone had fallen into the drapes that had concealed a closet. One end of the pole they had hung from rested on the sofa, and a couple copulated on the closet floor. Jack's drunkenness had become obvious.

"Are you about ready to go home?" Herb asked.

"Yes, I'll get my coat."

We said our good-byes, and Jack walked us to the door rather unsteadily, his arm around Herb's shoulder.

"Have t' have a drink sometime," he told Herb.

"Sure," Herb said.

"He's not your old man?" he asked me.

"Nope." My confident answer defiantly echoed Herb's.

"Well, 'night m' li'l chickadee," he said. Then he felt the need to explain, "'S doubla see feels."

It was a long walk downstairs. My legs were tired and shaky. Herb walked ahead of me and waited at the top of the concrete steps, at the heavy street door. He stood there like a beacon. The lights of home. I felt I'd never make it. Looking up at him, I put one foot on the bottom step.

"There's something strange about this night," I told him. "I feel like I'm trying to swim to shore, but I'm miles and miles off Cape Horn."

"Pounded by the Atlantic and Pacific, I suppose," he said. "Save your analogies for your literary friends. By the way, the building door's unlocked."

I shrugged, pushed open the big steel door, and went up the steps. Now I again stood in front of Bill's door, no, my door, and I groped in my pockets for the keys, spilling out old bus transfers and empty match books and the rock I'd been kicking earlier.

"Why don't you throw those things away?" Herb asked. "Are you collecting them or something?"

"Yeah," I answered. "Guess what?," I finally added tiredly. "No keys."

I saw them in my mind's eye, left behind on their nail when we went out the fire escape window.

Herb contemplated the door and asked, "Do you want me to break it down?"

Considering the alternative, I nodded, "Please!"

Herb stepped back as far as the bannister would allow and

threw his weight at the steel-covered door, ripping it off its hinges. It hung by a screw for a moment, then went over slowly, hitting the radiator with a final crash, like an exclamation point. We walked over it. The light from the hall made a path across the floor. Herb stood in it, asking "Do you think you'll be all right?"

I nodded.

"You don't want me to stay with you?"

I shook my head.

He stood the door up and slipped around it to the other side.

"Okay. Now push it in. I'll pull the doorknob from this side and try to set it in place."

I did, but it leaned a little. The hinges were too twisted to fit.

"Better prop something against it," he called to me from the other side of the door.

"I will."

"Good night."

I answered, "Good night." But it meant something more, something far more final, as I heard the words echo down the staircase.

Leaning against the door, I listened to his footsteps all the way down the stairs, listened to him close the building door carefully, so it would lock. My guts felt twisted like those hinges.

I don't need you. I don't need anyone.

I pushed a book case against the door, kicked my shoes across the room, pulled off my clothes, threw them against the wall, and fell into bed in utter darkness.

Chapter Nine

Light flooded the loft, touching my eyes warmly. I squinted at the clock. 12:15. As I lay there, pieces of here and now fit into place. Saturday. I'd have to get that door fixed. I'd go to Lu's and see if he and Jack could come help me with it. Jack would have stayed over; he was in no condition to leave.

And Herb; *don't think!*, I told myself. I willed the entire time we had known each other out of my memory. Everything from this day forward would have to be as it had been before we met. The spider had to go back inside the box.

Bill's loft was as it had been before his death, except for the presence of my sewing machine, and last night's clothes on the floor. I had changed nothing. I kicked the covers off, pulled on a robe, and went to the kitchen to make a pot of coffee.

The loft was huge, sixty feet by maybe thirty feet at the front and back ends, but the center lost some width to the stairwell, giving the whole apartment a squat U shape. There were no interior walls. Areas were designated by placement of the few pieces of furniture. The kitchen only gave an impression of being separated, because it was located at one end of the U. The center sleeping and sitting area was set apart from the kitchen and the large front studio by waist-high storage cabinets, which extended into the room at right angles to the wall. Between the cabinets were a double bed, with a red spread, a small oak table, and a chair, which Bill and I had re-webbed and reupholstered in blue plush the previous winter.

I showered, put on my jeans and an old sweater, and went over to Lu's. Jack had stayed the night, as I'd guessed. He and Lu stood in the kitchen, shivering, hung over, Jack's face and hair still wet from attempts at revitalization. Lu extracted cups from the dish drainer, saying "These are theoretically clean." The coffee was thick with grounds.

I explained my errand.

"Ha! Herb broke your door down!" Jack exclaimed. Both of them laughed uproariously, but I missed the humor.

"Man breaks down door in therapeutic vengeance!" Lu said, as if it were a headline.

"He broke it down at my request," I said, thinking they had misunderstood. "I had locked myself out."

"Just the same," said Jack, "I'm sure it did him good."

"Why?" I asked.

"That guy really looked hurt last night. Every time he looked at you he. . ."

"No! He wasn't!" I broke in. "He was disgusted with me. You just misinterpreted whatever you saw."

We headed for my place with Lu's tools to augment mine.

"Hey! You look good in jeans too," Jack remarked.

I smiled, a bit primly perhaps. I wasn't feeling as cocky as I had last night.

Lu hammered the hinges flat, and between the three of us we got the door up. Between the two of us, actually. Jack got in the way more than he helped. Lu left, Jack stayed and I heated up the coffee.

"Ah, thanks," Jack said as he sipped. "I was getting tired of those grounds."

"What was that business about your mom last night?" I asked. "Does she really dislike all your friends?"

"Nah, she just doesn't like Allen. Won't let me bring him home anymore. But of course I see him whenever I want."

"Where's home?"

"Richmond Hill. Queens."

"And you take care of your mom?"

"Well, my dad's dead and my brother died when I was little. I'm all she's got except for my sister, and she's married, so I feel responsible."

"I think that's commendable."

"You do? My friends think it's terrible." Jack's speech was unusual, carefully enunciated but carelessly structured. I thought I heard traces of an accent. His vowels were elongated, as in "Yoo doo" and "seee." Consonants at word endings were abrupt and pronounced, except for "r," which was inconsistent.

"Is Kerouac a French name?" I asked him.

"French Canadian. My folks moved from Quebec to Lowell, Massachusetts, and that's where I was brought up."

"That accounts for your 'r' then. Sometimes it sounds like Boston. Do you speak French?"

"Yeah, Canuck French. It's about as different from Parisian French as American is from the King's English." He paused, chin in hand. "Say, I could use something to eat. How 'bout you? Want to go out and have some breakfast?"

"I'm hungry too," I realized. "No need to go out though. There's plenty here. Do you feel like eggs? Toast?"

"Got any bacon? If you don't I'll go down and get some."

"I have bacon." We took our coffee to the kitchen and Jack sat on the car seat which, combined with a low table, served as a breakfast nook.

"Scrambled?" I asked. "Fried?"

"Scrambled will be great!"

I lay the strips of bacon in the pan and the aroma quickly filled the kitchen. Jack sniffed the air.

"Ah, that smells good! What do you do anyway? Do you work someplace?"

"Yes, I work in a funny place. I sew for a woman who has a dress shop. She has a queen complex."

"How's that?"

"We've all been instructed to answer her with 'Yes, Victoria' and 'No, Victoria' and practically bow to her when there are customers. We must show inordinate respect."

"She doesn't deserve it?"

"Not in my book. She's a fraud. Buys flawed merchandise, seconds and irregulars, for a song, and pawns them off as original creations ostensibly designed by her and executed by us, her seamstresses."

"What do you do then, to the dresses I mean?"

"We disguise the flaws, sort of redesign them in whatever ways occur to us. Sometimes we use two dresses of the same fabric to make a new one."

"Then *you're* the designers. You're being exploited!"

I just smiled. Breakfast done, I put it on the table and sat down.

"Oh, boy, does that look good!" Jack made anticipatory noises. "Um, ooh, ah, hmm. Hey, you're really amazing! You cook, you sew and you keep this place nice and tidy. You're a woman! Do you know women are a vanishing species?"

"Species?"

"Well, I mean real women. They're vanishing from this earth."

"Oh, I don't know about that," I objected. "Most women cook and a lot of women sew."

"Not any that I've run into lately." He dug into his breakfast with gusto. I had sliced some tomatoes to fill up the plate and add color, and there was strawberry jam for the toast.

"I must admit I do all right with breakfast, but I just go to pieces over anything complicated." I wanted to nip his illusion in the bud. "I can't even make a decent pie crust."

"Listen," he said, waving his fork. "Why don't you open your own shop?"

Here it comes, I thought. Everyone I meet has a new suggestion as to how I might constructively imprison myself.

"If your boss can make money off you," he continued, "why don't you do it yourself?"

"I'm not interested enough in it to make it a life's work."

"What are you interested in?"

"Everything!" I laughed. "If you apply the principles you use in solving design problems to more important and abstract issues, you're likely to come up with something quite worthwhile."

Jack just looked blankly across at me. "Is there any more coffee?" he asked.

I shook the coffee pot, poured the remains into his cup, and washed the pot so I could make some more. Two subjects were safe so far: his book and my domesticity.

"What about the book you're working on now?" I asked. "Tell me a little about it."

"Oh, it's a big rambling thing, just like this country. But a lot of it is about my friend Neal. What a guy!" He laughed. "You'll have to meet him. On second thought, maybe you shouldn't. He's had three wives already. You ever been married?"

"No."

"I was once, till her father got it annulled." He shook his head, laughing again. "Crazy dame. Absolutely crazy!"

He stretched out on the car seat and lit a cigarette, then asked with sudden inspiration, "Hey, you want to go to a movie tonight?"

"I don't know. Depends on the movie."

"'Death of a Salesman' is playing uptown. Have you seen it?"

"No. I'd like to."

"Well, I'm going back to Lu's for a while, have a few beers." He wiped his mouth and stood up. "How about if I come back here around seven? I'll see if Lu and Liz want to come with us."

"Okay, sounds fine."

"Thanks for the breakfast. It was great." He rubbed his stomach and started toward the door. I walked with him and was about to say goodbye, when he turned back abruptly.

"Lu says you didn't go to Bill's funeral," he burst out.

I nodded slowly. "That's right. I didn't."

"Didn't you want to pay your respects?"

"What does that mean?" Suddenly I felt bitter. "Would it show respect to go and stare at his empty body, to look at his maimed and repaired head? What kind of respect would that be?"

"But his family!"

"Oh, I'm sure they had enough New York nuts to contend with in their grief. They probably even felt his friends contributed to his death. They didn't miss me."

"Did you know them?"

"Yes. But." I saw Bill's mother, scratching her hands in her immaculate kitchen in Schenectady. *If I could cry, I'd cry for them, not for Bill.* "I don't think I want to talk about it."

"Okay. Sorry I brought it up."

"It's all right. It's just sort of pointless to talk about it now. It might have made some sense before he died."

"To talk about his funeral?"

"No, his parents."

He looked at me, puzzled, and finally turned toward the door. "Well, see you at seven," he said.

***

I did the dishes and then called my friend Sarah, because I hadn't seen her in weeks. I had joined her in her strange but wonderful apartment when I had left Herb. The toilet was under the entrance steps to the building, a real-life outhouse. The stone walls and dirt floor of the little room were anachronistic, not only in time but in place. But the address was perfect: 36 Park Avenue.

It was good to hear her voice, its little-girl-yodeling quality, like Shirley Temple's, and her faint laughter, as though she didn't have the strength for anything heartier. Sarah was an enigma to me. I knew she had great inner strength, firmness and conviction, yet she demonstrated only vagueness and fragility. She was possibly the only girl in Manhattan who was thinner than I was and still ambulatory. Her brown hair, so long that when she let it down it could have covered her as a garment, was worn in a classic Grecian coiled braid at the back of her head. In spite of this confinement, wayward wisps made little curls on her forehead and in front of her ears. A pencil line on the lids of her dark eyes was the only embellishment she took time for, but even this was unnecessary. It was a wonder to me that anyone so beautiful could be real.

We traded some significant bits of information about mutual friends and mutual interests, and decided to meet Monday night at the Pin Up Club, where her lover Walter Ruben played the piano.

I had planned to weatherstrip the windows, but there wasn't enough time to get it done before 7:00, so I sat down with Jack's book. I read a few paragraphs, then skimmed for several pages to get the feeling of his style. I decided that his descriptive passages were impressive, and I snuggled into my chair, getting set to read in earnest. But I lost interest after the second page, and closed the book, and looked at the wall. This was just the wrong time to try to read, because the Japanese fish kite had been in the loft all day, occupying the gigantic expanse of undecorated oyster-white wall.

I had first been visited by the kite six years before, when I had abruptly become aware of it, moving across the wall of my bedroom in Albany. It had been a muggy afternoon, unbearably hot, and I was laying on my bed, not moving, looking at a water stain on the wallpaper. As I watched, unfocused, the stain became a Japanese paper kite, turquoise and fuchsia and white, with black scalloped lines indicating the fish's scales. I savored the hallucination, allowing the black lines to leave the fish and become a grid on the wall. The fish swam across the grid and began to disintegrate, colors and paper and string all billowing into the atmosphere. The wall became the sky and the grid wavered and vanished. Colors broke down into atoms and merged with the sky, paper separated into fluff and solid, fluff disappeared into nothingness, while the solid formed itself into two spinning disks. I let the kaleidoscope go on and on, and I knew it could go on forever, no end and no beginning.

* * *

Jack arrived on time, by way of the fire escape, and we left immediately, hurrying along to the 23rd Street subway entrance. On the subway, Jack described everything and everybody like a tour guide.

"Now you see that little old guy sitting at the end there? Probably has a wife at home who made him wear that muffler. Can't you just hear her? 'It's cold out tonight, Henry'... or Egbert. Yeah, that would be his name... Egbert. 'Egbert, you wear your muffler, you hear me?' That's what she'd say." He nudged me, laughing. "And this girl behind us. She's tired. Been working on a Saturday, bringing home a little extra to feed her children. No old man to take care of her. Ah me!" He went on and on like this, and there was no denying that it was entertaining, but I only smiled.

My own view was that the muffler was Egbert's favorite, and his wife had been trying to get it away from him for years to give it to the Salvation Army. But Jack was looking for neither competition in storytelling nor exchange of opinions. He was perceiver and interpreter, the weaver of plots and intrigues, and he was in his element.

Though I listened and smiled, I must have left something to be desired in the way of an audience, for Jack asked me as we exited from the subway, "Don't you ever laugh?"

"Yes, I think I do."

"You're so quiet. So serious. Is something wrong?"

"No, no, I enjoyed your stories. I'm sorry if I didn't laugh."

He moped along toward the theater, making me think of what Steen had said about hurting people. I asked, "Jack, why do you care whether I laugh or not?"

"You make me feel that I'm not fun to be with."

"Oh, but you are! I haven't had so much fun in a long time." I could handle that. I'd try to laugh more.

"Hey, look!" he cried suddenly, running ahead. "Watch this!" He stood on his head in front of the theater just as the doors opened to spill out the earlier moviegoers. The contents of his pockets rolled in every direction and his tie fell over his nose. Pedestrians, caught off guard by this clown in their midst, bumped into each other in chain reaction. They weren't laughing, but I was, as Jack scrambled to pick up keys and change.

"Now I know how to make you laugh," he said with satisfaction, pulling me to the ticket window and straightening his jacket. "Any time I see you looking too serious, that's what I'll do."

* * *

My mother called Sunday afternoon to ask if I'd be coming upstate for Thanksgiving. I hadn't thought about it, hadn't really realized Thanksgiving was so close.

"Make it a one-way ticket this time, dear," she urged. "There's no reason for you to be away from your family."

"But I've got a good job!" I protested. I argued with her and finally promised to call next weekend to make definite holiday plans.

I should have told her truthfully that I didn't want to live as a daughter at her home anymore, but it seemed a harsh and heartless thing to say. I couldn't think of a diplomatic way to put it. I thought of Bill's petite beautiful mother, just as I had when Jack asked me why I didn't attend the funeral. She had been educated at the Sorbonne. I thought of how she had looked up at me with sad dark eyes while we topped and tailed green beans in her spotless Schenectady kitchen. "Is he still drinking... as much?" she had asked, trying not to scratch her eczema. "The doctor says it's nerves," she'd added, as she saw me staring at her raw hands.

The best I could do for my mother, for her peace of mind, was to describe my job as much better than it was, my apartment safer and more attractive, and my activities more conventional, wholesome as fresh milk. Since I was neither married nor going to school, a good job would have to suffice as my reason for staying here. In my heart, though, I knew that now that Bill was dead and I had broken up with Herb, my only real reason for staying was that I hadn't decided where to go next.

I had been a file clerk, a dental assistant, a model, a waitress, a receptionist, and a sales clerk, and my mother had never yet been proud of me. "You have a good head on your shoulders," she had once said to me. "I'd like to see you use it." And in response to that, I came up with a job as a hair model in a beautician's school.

Now, one of the pleasures of my job as a seamstress/designer was that my mother seemed pleased about my choice. That had never happened before.

Victoria, my boss, was more than satisfied with both the quality and quantity of my work, and she allowed me to step out the back door whenever I pleased. No one looked over my shoulder. I was responsible to myself to do the best job I could, and I did, and I took home no headaches or business worries. Elena and Maria were lovely co-workers, both from Puerto Rico, and the fact that there were no men to harass us made the job just about perfect.

The way I saw it, I was given free materials to challenge my imagination and abilities. I worked things out on my boss's time, and got paid besides. I was humored in my refusal to work with synthetics. I understood the properties of natural fibers, silk, wool, cotton, and linen. But these new materials of coal, glass, oil and chemicals were cold, dead, and brittle. Fortunately, Elena and Maria didn't mind them.

Mitering corners, easing sleeves into armholes, and making darts at angles all seemed to me to bear some relation to larger questions in my mind, and I never tired of looking for parallels between sewing and philosophical problems.

Lately I had been thinking a lot about the use of backings for flimsy fabrics. A silk chiffon simply will not tailor unless it is backed. I chose not to use it in patterns which wouldn't utilize its own inherent ethereal quality. Why force it into a role it could not assume naturally, when nothing else could ever do what silk does best?

The aspect of resiliency had also been fascinating me recently. The warp and woof (the straight lines of the goods) have no give, but the diagonal (bias) is so flexible it becomes wavy and ripply. It will expand and contract and will conform to just about any shape. I delighted in finding political implications in that idea.

As I stitched arrow-shaped miters into place for reinforcement,

I invented football plays, moved army battalions, and swayed public opinion. And I was much happier doing it in my own imagination than I ever could have been playing roles like those in the real world.

Chapter Ten

Jack's voice called from the street late Sunday night. I wasn't pleased as I walked sleepily across the loft to the window. I had told him I'd have things to do and needed some time just to be alone. I opened my window and called down in irritation, "I have to work tomorrow!"

"I won't stay," he shouted back. "I want to tell you something." Our voices shattered the silence of the deserted street. I threw the keys down and opened the loft door. In seconds he was upstairs.

"What is it?" I asked, standing in the doorway, holding my bathrobe together.

"Just a minute. Let me sit down at least." I stood while he sat and caught his breath.

"Come sit down," he said. "I told you I won't stay, only listen, I came all the way into the city to tell you this."

"Why didn't you call?"

"Because I don't know your number and I don't even know your last name. I could have called Lu to find out, but that's beside the point. I wanted to see you to tell you this. You make me nervous standing in the doorway. Come on, sit down. I'll leave in five minutes, all right?"

I gave up my post and sat down, apologizing, "Look, I'm sorry to be this way but I really do have to get some sleep." Jack was bursting with confidence and spirit, with none of the poutiness and charming bashfulness I'd seen in the last two days. "Listen," he said, "I got to thinking about you last night when I got home, and I thought about you all day today. I even told my mom about you. I want to marry you."

"What?" I caught my breath. "What... what on earth for?" I finally managed to ask in disbelief.

"What does anyone get married for? To have a home together. To have children. To grow old."

"But why me? We just met! We don't even know each other."

"We have the rest of our lives to get to know each other. And I know I want you to be my wife. Now what I was thinking is this..." He gestured agitatedly, laying it out for me. "You can quit your job. We'll both get part time jobs and do what we want with the rest of the time. I'll finish my book and you can do whatever you want. Sew things or whatever."

"Hey! Wait a minute. How do you know I want to be married?"

"I know you want to have children, and getting married is still the best way to do that."

"How do you know I want children?"

"Bill told me. He told me a lot about you. So you see, I know you better than you thought. Say, have you got any coffee made? I could sure use a cup."

"Yes, there's coffee and it's still hot." I went to get it. I had suddenly developed an interest in what he had to say. I poured a cup for myself too, putting aside my resolve to get a good night's sleep, and setting our coffee on the small table, I asked, "What did Bill tell you about me?"

"I told him what kind of girl I was looking for and he said I had described you perfectly. Only trouble is, he called you Cathy. That threw me off the other night when I met you. It wasn't until today that I realized why Liz called you Cathy. And then, I thought you and Bill had been having an affair because Allen said he'd seen the two of you running around in nothing but sheets."

I smiled, remembering the afternoon we'd doused each other with water pistols on the neighborhood rooftops, costumed as movie Arabs. "No. That was just... playing."

"What did Bill tell you about me?" Jack asked.

"He said you were a writer. Also called you a *'mensch.'*"

"Oh, he did?" Jack seemed pleased.

I nodded, but my forehead was creased in a frown. "But Jack, regardless of what he told either of us, I think it's important that we remember that no two people are going to describe someone else in the same way. I see you as very boyish, not like a *mensch* at all."

"No? I think he was right about *you*!"

"But he was drunk! He never called me Cathy except when he was drunk."

"But so was I," Jack admitted. "So maybe we understood each other on that level. Why did he call you Cathy?"

"Because he was Heathcliff."

"And you weren't lovers?"

"Cathy and Heathcliff weren't lovers. They were companions."

"But they would have been, if Cathy hadn't married Roger Linden."

"That was a different Cathy."

"No it wasn't!"

"For Bill it was," I insisted.

"When I told Bill about the girl I was looking for, the wife of my dreams, he said I had described Cathy perfectly."

"How did you describe the girl you were looking for?"

"A sweet little, nice little home-type girl, just like you. Not clever or witty, not worldly or jaded, and. . ." Jack paused, embarrassed. "And not forward, you know? Not a man chaser."

"Oh. Yes. I know." I mulled that over, wondering if sensuality or the lack of it had entered their discussion. Jack was refreshingly unaggressive. "Did you tell him you were looking for a girl who cooked and sewed?"

"Yeah! He said you were a great cook!"

"He taught me just about everything I know about cooking."

Jack smiled. "You know, I can't wait for you to meet my mom. She's got these big blue, innocent eyes. You'll love her."

I stared at him, suddenly enchanted by his voice. "Beeg bloo," he had said. For a moment, it almost made me shiver.

"What about your mom?" I asked. "What would she do if you married?"

"Aw, she doesn't need me. I use her as an excuse so I never have to stay in one place too long."

I laughed. "What would you use for an excuse if you were married? Your wife?"

"If I were married to you, I wouldn't be in places where I'd need an excuse. I'd be home with you, or you'd be with me."

"Why?" I asked.

"Because I love you!"

I must have looked appalled. "Don't say things like that!" Calmly, I followed with, "I don't think you've probably ever loved anybody. But believe me, I don't mean that disparagingly."

"What are you talking about?"

"I mean that if I say no, it won't be for that reason."

"But you won't say no," Jack insisted. "Think of it! We'll save some money, buy an old truck and go across this whole big old country. And we'll live next to Neal and Carolyn. And we'll have babies, lots and lots of. . ."

I stopped him. It felt insane to even listen to this. "Why don't we just see how we feel about this in a few months, Jack? You'll have to admit this would take some thinking about. You're not in a hurry, are you?"

"Yes, I am! There's no time to waste. You quit your job and we'll go get the license tomorrow. I'm afraid you'll marry someone else!"

"Not a chance," I smiled. "Of all the men who've proposed to me today, I like you best."

"You know," he said defensively, "someday I'm going to be a big author. I'll make lots of money. And you really shouldn't be living in this place all alone. It's not safe."

"Aha! You want me for my loft. I knew there was a catch," I laughed. "There are quite a few noses out of joint over my living here anyway."

"Allen says you want to make a shrine of the place. 'A vulturish shrine,' he said."

"Really! Allen said that? Now who is more vulturish than Allen? That's probably what he would do."

"I wouldn't be surprised." Jack put his empty cup down and looked at me. "Now just be a sweet girl," he said, "and tell me you'll marry me so I can go tell Lu I'll be his neighbor."

"You've got a bet on with Lu, is that it? I can't take you seriously, Jack."

"You've got to take me seriously. Or I'll set up housekeeping outside your door."

"Oh, you will?" I laughed again. "Last night you were looking for ways to make me laugh."

"Yeah, all I have to do is ask you to marry me. That's good for laughs, right?" There was an edge to his voice.

"You better check to see if Lu's home before it gets too late. And I've got to get to bed."

"Doesn't matter if he's not home," Jack said petulantly. "I've got a key." He put on his jacket, lit a cigarette, and stood up to leave. "I'll come to meet you tomorrow night after work."

"No. I won't be here," I said. "I'm meeting a girlfriend after work. Wednesday night at the earliest."

"What time are you getting home? This is no neighborhood to come home alone to after dark."

"I always take a cab," I said, shrugging.

"I want to call you tomorrow night." He stood at the head of the stairs, his hand on the bannister. "What time?"

"I'll be home at ten."

"I'll call you. G'night." He ran down the stairs.

"Wait! Jack?"

He stopped and turned back. "Yeah?"

I hesitated, not sure why I had yelled to him to wait. "Please close the door carefully to be sure it locks."

Chapter Eleven

Monday morning was dreary and cold. I hurried to Victoria's shop through the bone-chilling November sleet, ran up the steps onto the loading platform, and through the back door to the little room with its three sewing machines.

Elena had arrived early, and she looked up from threading to ask me brightly, "*Hace frío, no* (it's cold, isn't it)?"

"*Bastante frío para mi* (plenty cold for me)," I agreed. I stood by the steam press, warming myself, looking into the front of the shop to see the nattily-dressed gentleman who sat all day looking out the front door. His white gloved hands rested on top of the cane that he always held between his knees and his shiny black shoes. He never left his chair and never took off his gloves. The other seamstresses and I speculated endlessly on his function. Was he Victoria's backer? Her paramour? Maybe the shop was a 'front' and he was posted by the door as a lookout. When Victoria sat beside him, she spoke in soothing tones, unlike the strident voice she used for us or the haughty one she reserved for her customers.

Victoria was not the typical Village shopkeeper. Middle-aged with dyed black hair and makeup well toward the heavy side, she wore corsets under her pedestrian clothing. As Maria came in stamping her feet and pulling off her scarf, Victoria imperiously began to impart the orders for the day, crossing the red carpet of the shop to stand on the linoleum floor of the back room.

"The orange silk is a must! I want that for the window tomorrow. Who will do it?"

Elena examined the dress, saw the machine oil spots down the side of the skirt, and volunteered.

"Now, the brown wool. Something must be done with this! Joan, I think this is a job for you." She showed me the slash pockets, with narrow frayed seams coming apart. The same thing was happening to the neckline. I took the garment and hung it in my work area.

"The green suit is yours, then, Maria." The green suit's problem was a flaw in the fabric itself, and Maria's eyes went to the rack of clothing that ran the length of an entire wall, searching for something of an identical fabric.

"Work on whatever you want when you have time left over." Victoria left the room.

I looked over my project, and finally decided to face the pockets and neckline with something decorative but substantial. I began rummaging through our scrap boxes.

"Maria," I asked. "*Adonde aprendistes a coser* (where did you learn to sew)?"

"*En casa, y tu* (at home, and you)?"

"English spoken here!" Victoria called from the front of the shop.

"I'm sorry, I forgot," I said.

"Yes, Victoria!" she corrected.

"Yes, Victoria," I assented.

I sighed. The conversation would go much slower in English. This new rule had gone into effect last week when the three of us had burst into laughter over the possible reason for the old man's white gloves.

"*Porque nunca sacalos, los guantes* (why doesn't he ever take those gloves off)?" Elena had asked.

"*En por eso*," I'd answered, "*tiene manos verdes*. (Maybe he has green hands.)"

Perhaps Victoria had been afraid we were making fun of her. Whatever it was, the sound of laughter coupled with us speaking a language she didn't understand was upsetting enough to make her put an end to use of the foreign tongue altogether.

Maria continued in English now.

"And you? You learn in school?"

"No," I told her. "I learned at home, too."

"I think American girls learn everything in school. Even to cook," she said. "But you learn at home. From your mother?"

"No. From myself. How about you, Elena?"

"At home everybody sew," Elena explained. "You want some clothes, you sew. You want some food, you cook. My mother, my grandmother, aunts, cousins, sisters, everybody sew. I watch, I sew a little bit, I learn."

Elena was a master at putting in godets and other tricky inserts, and I watched her now with the orange silk.

"Did you learn to do that by watching?" I asked her.

"Oh no," she laughed. "I learn this from myself."

* * *

The dress was done by noon. I created the illusion of an entire lining of coffee-colored satin, just by facing the pockets, neckline, and sleeves with a few scraps. Satisfied that it could fill somebody's holiday needs with elegance, I hung it in the front of the shop so Victoria could put a price tag on it.

After lunch I took my reward in the form of a gray silk chiffon

I had been waiting to get my hands on. It was a long gown with a rip in the skirt near the hem, and I wanted to applique black lace in a border and then cut away the chiffon behind it. I knew where there was such a piece of lace, and I went to get it, a beautiful length of Alencon. As I spread out the skirt on my work table and laid the lace over it, Elena and Maria exclaimed over it.

"A hundred dollars!" Maria cried.

"*Por lo menos* (at least)!" concurred Elena. "Oh, I like to have dress like that!"

"Do you ever go to the thrift shops? The Salvation Army?" I asked them.

Elena was too new to the country to have heard of them.

"*Ropa usada* (used clothes)," Maria whispered to her.

"So what if they're used?" I asked. "You can find stuff like this for a dollar or two."

"But old!" Maria objected. "And some people wore it."

"It's not all old. Rich people give their clothes away. They just get tired of them. And at Bloomingdale's some people wore the clothes, too. To try them on."

"I like to see it," Elena said. She was probably the sole support of her family.

"I'll take you some Saturday. Maybe this Saturday if you can."

"Maybe if you come, tell my father, he let me go," she suggested.

"Sure. Give me your address."

She started to write it on the back of an envelope, then realized her address was on the other side.

"It's here!" She pointed to an address in Spanish Harlem and gave me the envelope.

"Maybe I go too, if my husband let me," Maria weakened.

"I have to bring my brother," Elena apologized.

"I don't mind! He'll probably find something at the thrift shops too."

Elena's brother dropped her off every morning on his way to vocational trade school, and came back to take her home every night. Maria and her husband lived in the housing project by the East River. He worked at the dry cleaners next door, and not only escorted her to and from work but spent his lunch hour with her as well. How protected these girls were! I didn't envy them, not at all.

* * *

At five o'clock, I stuffed my thermos into my bag and hurried uptown to meet Sarah. She wasn't in front of the Pin Up, so I walked over to Park Avenue, expecting to run into her.

About a block from her building, I saw her strolling down the avenue as though there were no such thing as time, pencil-slim yet willowy and graceful, a fashion photographer's dream. She wore an impeccably tailored brown suit with a geranium-colored scarf at the neck, and she walked as confidently and comfortably in spiked heels as she would have in bare feet. Carrying a thin, black umbrella jauntily like a walking stick, she gazed up at the second-story windows of the building as she passed. She was so engrossed was she that she didn't see me till I was almost next to her.

"What's up there that's so interesting?"

"Oh!" she cried, startled. "It's a men's club. Didn't you ever notice all those men looking out the windows? Rich old men. I always look to see who'll wink at me."

"Naughty girl!" I chided. But I looked up and sure enough, several white-haired gentlemen smiled down at us, and one winked at me.

"I got a wink, Sarah!"

"Naughty girl!" She gave me a little push with her shoulder. "My mother used to say, 'Will you be an old man's darling or a young man's sweetheart?'"

"Why the interest in old men?" I asked.

"Well, when you stop and think about it, it makes a lot of sense. Not for you, maybe. You've got Herb."

I shook my head. "It's all finished."

"I don't believe it!" she said as we walked into the Pin Up.

We sat on the black upholstered divan along the window, next to the piano. Walter was just finishing "Smoke Gets In Your Eyes." He played with eyes appropriately half-closed, avoiding the smoke from the cigarette hanging between his lips. He lifted his eyebrows and smiled lazily at us. We'd both known him since the summer before.

The waiter took our order for cocktails as Walter left the piano to join us. "Put those on my bill," Walter told the waiter. "These are my two favorite girls." He gave Sarah and me a brief hug, one arm for each of us.

"Hello, Sarah. How are you, Pablo?" I never knew why he called me Pablo.

Sarah single-mindedly pursued the subject I'd rather have dropped. "Didn't you and Herb get back together after you left my place? This was eight months ago! I thought you were seeing each other again."

"We were, but... we just antagonize each other. We're too different, and I've finally realized it's a destructive relationship."

"Opposites attract," Walter said.

"Yes," I agreed. "Differences are what brought us together and made it dynamic. But they also drove us apart."

"Can't you just agree to live with the differences?" Sarah asked.

"I could, maybe, but he... he doesn't even want me. I don't come up to his standards. Intellectually, educationally, any way at all."

"Yes, he does want you, Pablo," Walter insisted. "I saw him

after you left him and moved in with Sarah. He was in here, drinking."

"Drinking? Herb?"

"Yes, and he was in pretty bad shape over the whole thing."

"Well, he never gave *me* any indication that I was anything other than a disappointment to him. And I don't need that. I've got a mother to be disappointed in me."

"He only wants what's best for you."

"I've got a mother for that too!" I laughed. "Don't you see, Walter? I don't need another mother. I need a partner!"

"He reached you, at least. You know I didn't think anyone ever could."

"No one ever will again," I said firmly. "I don't ever want to be that vulnerable again."

"You sound bitter, Joan. Maybe you should consider an old man too," Sarah suggested.

I smiled. "But an old man might not give me children. And that's the only use I'd have for a man, now."

"People pay for stud service, Pablo!" Walter said.

"Oh, I'm going to pay, Walter. You know that. You know it's going to cost me dearly."

Walter smiled as he stood up to go back to the piano. "What are your requests?" he asked. "I'll play one for each of you."

"'Once in a While,'" I said. "Stardust" was Sarah's choice.

While Walter played, Sarah returned to expounding on the advantages of older lovers. "They're gentle and patient," she said. "So much more relaxed."

I thought back to Clarence and Cliff and told her, "I've known a couple who were just as aggressive as high school boys."

"Past sixty, I think, is best," Sarah mused. "That's when they stop trying to prove they can still perform as well as young men."

"You sound like you've made a study of the sex life of the older male."

"I have," Sarah answered. "You think I'm joking, but I'm through with young men."

"But don't you want a family? And aren't men of that age impotent?"

"No, I don't want children. If I did, yes, I'd want a man who would live long enough to help me raise them. But this impotency thing, I think it's a myth."

"You do?"

"There's a big difference between being impotent and just not being able to get it up as often. But this idea that impotence goes hand in hand with old age is so ingrained that the first time a man experiences failure, it's frightening enough that he'd rather forget the whole thing than go through the ordeal again."

"Then at least their wives get a rest in their old age."

"Now, *there's* a paradox!" she exclaimed. "I think that older women are more aggressive and more easily aroused. I hear the most terrible tales about demanding wives! And of course, the more pressured the poor man feels, the less capable he is of performing."

"If that's true, then it sounds like Mother Nature goofed. How can such an unbalanced situation be natural?"

"It wouldn't be unbalanced, but people play such self-defeating games. You watch a middle-aged couple, even socially, they get themselves locked into this syndrome where she attacks his manhood and he attacks her physical appearance. If they do that publicly, with little verbal jabs, just think how they must harm each other in the intimacy of their bed."

"I never thought about that at all," I said.

Sarah began to get wound up. "Middle age is the time when the male begins to have worries about his job performance. Whether or not he'll lose his position to a younger man, right? He begins to have doubts about his achievements, thinks he should have gone further, should have done more. And now he's got all these worries about his manhood to contend with as well.

"His wife, on the other hand," Sarah went on, "has probably said goodbye to the last of her children, doesn't feel as necessary as she once did, and she's finding wrinkles and having trouble keeping the weight down."

"It's terribly sad," I agreed.

"But now look at what they do to each other out of ego and pride. Just when they need moral support the most, they cut each other down. He tells her she doesn't excite him any more, to relieve himself of the responsibility of satisfying her. And she tells him he couldn't do anything about it even if she were Lana Turner!"

"After all those years of preparing for the future," I said, "they've blown it."

"But it doesn't have to be that way at all. I mean, let's face it, in bed, the preliminaries are the best part. That's *got* to be true for most women. And the nice thing is, with an older man that can go on for days because he's slower to arouse. But I am a young woman, still naturally passive, and maybe it keeps me from going to the lengths an older man needs. And that's where the balance comes in: an older, more aggressive woman would be better able to satisfy those needs, if only those couples could just let their old roles go and accept the new ones."

I looked at her, smiling. "Sarah, I'm really impressed by how much you've thought and learned about the subject."

Walter returned to the table. "I keep telling her she should study geriatrics," he said to me.

"And I keep telling him, that's what I am doing! Why should I go to school to study things that are right in front of me?"

* * *

As Sarah and I walked back to her apartment, I was thinking about natural passivity, about whether there were men our age who were less sexually aggressive, about impotence as a result of pressure to perform.

"My friend Connie and her date were in her apartment," I told Sarah, "and she was getting tired of fighting him off. . ."

"What did she let him in for?" Sarah immediately wanted to know. "She must have known what he wanted."

"Oh yes. They'd been having an affair. But she wasn't feeling cooperative on this particular night, you know? And the way she told the story, she was tired of fighting so she just pulled up her skirt, spread her legs and said, 'All right, damn it! Go ahead and just take it!' And he lost it right then and there. And he never could get it up with her again."

"My God! How awful!" Sarah said. "I could never do a thing like that. Could you?"

"Emasculate a man? Well, not under normal circumstances, but since she told me the story, I've been wondering about the use of it in a rape situation."

"Do you worry about that too?" she asked. "I've had a couple of close calls just in the past few weeks."

"What would you do, Sarah? What would you do?"

"I think I'd give in," she mused. "It would be too hard to figure out what sort of quirky personality I was dealing with. You just never know what's going to arouse a stranger. What would you do, Joan?"

I shivered. "I just hope I never have to find out. On high school dates I used to say I was going to be sick. That always got the car door open. Nobody wants to be thrown up on. But I think I'd be able to outwit a rapist. I really do."

We arrived at Sarah's wrought iron gate and she invited me inside for sandwiches and a can of soup. As we heated the soup,

I confessed my reason for wanting to see her tonight.

"I need a roommate, Sarah," I said. "That loft is so big two people could live in it and never see each other. You have to come and see it."

"Oh, Joan. I couldn't leave this place. I'm really attached to it. I'll come and visit you a lot, though. Why don't you put an ad in the paper?"

"I'm too fussy about who I live with, I think." I sighed. "I knew you wouldn't want to give up your place but it was worth a try. Remember when we used to cook our morning oatmeal in this fireplace?"

"That was fun! I never used to eat breakfast until you came here. I used to pretend that I was a little girl and you were my mommy, fixing breakfast."

I smiled. Then, "Oh, I forgot to tell you!" I burst out. "I was proposed to last night! By a man who sees me as a domestic, a great cook and housekeeper, and a sweet little homebody."

"Bring him around," she said. "I'll set him straight. I'll tell him how you used to ruin my eggs. Who is he? What does he do?"

"Jack Kerouac. Does that ring a bell?"

Sarah shook her head.

"I wouldn't have known who he was, either, except Bill used to talk about him last summer. He's a writer. At least, he's written one book, and he's at work on another."

"Have you read his book?"

"Uh-uh, except for a few pages. Every time I turn around, he's there, and for some reason he's determined to get married."

"How long have you known him?"

"I just met him last Friday night. I really don't know much about him. He's French Canadian and lives on Long Island with his mother. I expect he's been spoiled."

"Oh dear," Sarah lamented. "Please don't get involved with a mama's boy. Nothing but bad news."

"Who's getting involved? He's the one who wants to get married."

"Yes, and you're the one who needs a roommate," Sarah pointed out. "Is the loft going to be difficult to afford by yourself?"

"Oh no, that's not the reason. I really like living alone. It's the safety factor, Sarah."

"Maybe this guy just wants you for the loft."

"I thought that at first, but he talks about getting a truck and going to San Francisco. And in some ways, I like the idea of leaving New York. I don't trust myself not to call Herb."

"You're not over it, then," Sarah said.

"I never will be," I admitted. "But there's no going back, Sarah. It's really finished."

* * *

Sarah invited me to stay the night. "You can take the Fifth Avenue bus down to work in the morning, and we can talk till we fall asleep, just like we used to."

"I would, Sarah, but I told Jack I'd be home at ten to get his call. I should be leaving soon."

"Let me show you something before you go. It's a suit I made. I'm going to try it on for you."

She stepped behind a screen, and emerged in a spectacular navy wool suit with a deep cowl neckline, filled in with a white lace jabot. "Ta—*da!*" she announced, stepping forth in her best fashion model's walk. She pivoted in front of me, walked away, then turned and unbuttoned the jacket so I could see the skirt. She had made darts from near the center of the waist band, and incorporated them into seams that extended diagonally out to the hip bones, then down in a plumb line. The result was a perfect fit with uncluttered lines.

"It's the suit of the year!" I said admiringly. "It says 'Spring 1951' all over it."

"I think I might get a show," she said proudly.

"*Really?*" I squealed. "Let me see what else you've done! Do you have a backer?"

"Yes, I have!" she said. Her excitement was apparent as she brought out more garments for my inspection. "A fifty-five-year old photographer."

"A mere youth!" I remarked, as I marvelled at her creations.

"Well, he is very mature for his age, and he's going through his difficult years gracefully. I expect great things of him in another ten years."

"Sarah, these are really out of the ordinary. The best you've done, I think. I expect great things of *you*, very soon!"

"I'm glad you like them. Six months of my life went into them."

"I'm very impressed, not only with the designs, but also the workmanship."

"Workmanship," Sarah sighed. "Now there's a problem if I have to fill orders. Who can do work like that? No school teaches detail like this."

"Don't fret. The two girls who work with me are just as good as you or me."

"Really? Where did they learn to sew?"

"*En casa, como sus madres y abuelas* (at home, like their mothers and grandmothers)."

"Oh great! But do you think they'd work for me?"

"Once they know you, there'll be no problem, Sarah. I'm taking them on a tour of the thrift shops Saturday. Maybe you would like to come along."

"I'll do it," she said.

"Call me then, and we'll decide where to meet." I looked at the clock. "I've got to go! Will you come out with me while I get a taxi?"

* * *

"Right here, driver," I instructed, a few minutes later. "Number 151."

"Here? In a factory?"

"The top floor is an apartment." I looked at the meter and paid him. The change would do for a tip.

"Doesn't look safe to me," the driver observed. "Want me to see you upstairs?"

"No, that's all right. They lock the doors at five, when the factory closes."

"I'll wait here till you get inside, then."

"Thanks." Key in hand, I ran to the door, unlocked it, and waved the cab away before shutting it and listening for the click that locked it. I took off my shoes, put them in with the groceries I'd picked up, and started up the stairs two at a time.

A little more than halfway up, I froze, hearing a noise like the rustling of paper coming from my floor. Could it be paper blowing against the roof door? Looking up the stairwell, I though I saw a movement at the top bannister.

I waited, considering my options. I was near the top, and I doubted my ability to outrun a pursuer down the stairs. And the thought of a roof chase at night was certainly unappealing. I decided that if there was somebody there, my best move would be to get both of us inside the loft, then watch for an opportunity to get out on the fire escape.

Still I listened, motionless, watching the bannister for several minutes, almost convincing myself that it had been my imagination. There was no way anyone could get into this building as long as the roof door was locked, and I could see, as I continued warily upward, that it was. *Even if there is somebody there,* I told myself, *it can only be another human being. Communication is always possible.*

But all my strength left me when I reached the landing and saw that there *was* somebody leaning against the wall by my door.

"Carl," I said unenthusiastically.

* * *

I had worked at Benny's Steak House for three days last month. Carl, the bartender, had been my reason for leaving.

Benny had sent me down to the cellar to get some lard, and I couldn't find the light switch in the dungeon of a place. The only light came from a soot-caked screen at the street end of the cellar, from that place under the sidewalk grating in front of the restaurant. The walls were damp stone, filled with crumbling mortar, and the floor was dirt. I didn't see how such a foundation could hold up the building.

Carl had come down the stairs into the filthy dark after me. "Can't find the light switch?" he asked. But instead of helping me, he closed the cellar door and pressed the tight muscular hardness of his body against mine, pinning me to the cool stone. My bones suddenly felt as fragile as a bird's.

Infuriated, and with an adrenaline rush, I attacked him, but my kicks and pushes seemed to just bring out a rush in him. The harder I fought and the more I struggled, the brighter his eyes gleamed, like a rat's in the dank darkness. He laughed softly, throatily, and I thought I would become a permanent part of the wall.

"Spunky, aren't you?" he hissed. "I like spunky, skinny girls."

Benny suddenly kicked open the cellar door and shouted down in irritation, "Carl! Make it snappy! You got a customer!"

Carl had smirked at me and promised, "I'll get you sooner or later."

And here he was to keep that promise. "Hello there, Spunky," he leered at me.

"What a surprise," I offered. I wasn't going to let him see my fear or anger. "How did you get through that locked door?"

"I been here since 4:30. Took a nap. Took a piss off your roof. Hope I din't hit nobody." The rustle of paper I had heard was from the bag around the bottle he held clutched in his hand. Judging from the way he looked and sounded, I guessed it must be nearly empty.

"I know you don't always get in so late, 'cause I been watchin'," he told me. "Big date tonight? Lemme see if you're still hot." He enveloped me with the same bone-crunching embrace, and I had the unwelcome taste of whiskey in my mouth. *Relax*, I told myself. *Go limp. Be dull.*

"Well, that's a change!" he said. "Feelin' friendlier tonight? Where's my spunky girl?"

"I'm too tired to fight," I said.

"Well then, ain't you gonna unlock your door?" I looked at it, surprised that it hadn't given way already with the weight of the two of us against it.

"No. I mean yes, if you want to wait inside for me," I said nervously. "I have to go back downstairs. Left the rest of my groceries. It was too much for one trip." I looked longingly at the shoes inside my bag, but I knew he'd buy the story more easily if I left them. Who'd run out in the cold without shoes?

"Leave the groceries. How'd you get 'em home?"

"Took a cab." That was an easy answer. "I can't leave them because it's mostly booze and someone will take it." I didn't know what he'd been drinking, or even if it made any difference.

"I'll come with you," he said. Reluctantly I started down the stairs. I wondered how he would react to the idea of an attached woman.

"We can drink to the success of my marriage," I told him.

"When you gettin' married?"

"Next week," I invented.

"Glad I din't wait no longer to come by."

We were almost on the ground floor, when "Hold on there!" Carl cried out. His suspicion was late in coming, but not late enough. "You left your groceries outside? That was a dumb thing to do!"

"I wasn't thinking. The bag was heavy and I just put it down to unlock the door. I didn't know I'd be upstairs so long."

"If you're playing games with me. . ."

"Why would I do that?" I had one hand on the latch. I was so close.

"Uh uh!" he yelled. "I'll do it." He pushed me back from the door and opened it just enough to see out. I rushed at the crack of freedom with all the power I had, but was stopped by an arm whacked against my chest and a hard slap on the side of my face.

"Bitch! Get up those stairs!"

"Somebody's taken them already!" I cried.

He hit me again, knocking me into the wall, yelling "Up those stairs!" And as I hung onto the bannister for support, he began to laugh softly, just as he had at Benny's. I suddenly knew that he wasn't angry, just trying to induce fear, because that was what aroused him.

He picked me up as if I weighed nothing, saying "This is quicker. I ain't got all night." My legs had turned to jelly, and I couldn't have walked up the stairs anyway. He set me in front of my door, where I would have collapsed if he hadn't had an iron grip on my arm.

"Your key," he demanded. I fished it out of my pocket and handed it to him. He unlocked the door and immediately pushed me toward the bed.

This is all crazy, I thought. *It can't be true.* I had never known fear, and now my teeth were chattering. *Why can't I stand outside this, be a spectator, turn it into a movie?*

And write a better script!

He was taking off his belt and appraising me. "Take off your clothes," he said coolly.

"Listen, Carl, this is a lousy idea. Come sit down beside me. I want to talk to you."

"Are you out of your mind? I said take off your clothes! Take them off or I'll rip them off you!"

The phone rang and I lunged for it. Carl flicked the belt and caught me on the leg. "Don't answer it," he said.

I looked, amazed, at what the belt had done to my nylons. I knew it would tear open my bare skin. But, "Carl, I have to answer it," I blurted. "It's my fiance calling to see if I got home safely."

"Where is he calling from?"

"The—the loft next door. He'll come over by the fire escape if I don't answer."

"Answer it." He stood listening, a hulking presence breathing near me, as I picked up the receiver with trembling fingers.

"Oh, Jack! Thank God!" I shouted into the phone.

Carl said quietly, "I'm gone," and went out the door.

Jack sounded puzzled. "Did you think I wasn't going to call?"

"I... thought I wasn't going to get to the phone in time." My heart beat so fast and loud I was sure he could hear it over the wire, and my breath came in gasps.

"What did you do? Run up the stairs?"

"Yes, I ran. Hold on a second while I close the door." I locked it quickly, then slipped back into place by the phone.

"Are you all right?" Jack asked. "You sound funny."

"Yes. Yes, I'm all right!" I was amazed that I was, still shaking, trying not to show it. "I'm perfectly all right and I'm awfully glad that you called."

"Well, that's something, at least. Did you have a good time with your friend tonight?"

"Yes, very good. She's a designer and she's going to have her own show soon. And she's a model." I babbled on while I felt the side of my face swelling. I examined the rest of myself for possible injuries.

"I'll come to see you tomorrow night," he said.

"Didn't we decide it would be Wednesday night?" I asked.

"Yeah. Wednesday. And Tuesday. And Thursday. Friday, Saturday, Sunday and Monday."

"Let's keep it Wednesday. I need a night to get caught up and get some sleep. I didn't get much sleep last night."

"Did you lie awake thinking of me?"

"You did give me a lot to think about, you know."

"Okay. I won't ask for tomorrow too. Wednesday it is, and I'll bring some stuff for dinner. How's that?"

"Fine, if you want to do that."

"And some wine. What kind of wine do you like?"

"Get whatever you like, Jack. I'm not much of a drinker."

"What time then? What time do you get off work?"

"Oh, let's make it around seven. That'll give me enough time to unwind."

"All right. I'll see you then." And he hung up. I went to the bathroom mirror to see what was happening to my face, and I was horrified. My left eye was almost swollen shut and a bluish color was already showing me where the bruises would be.

I was furious and humiliated. He had treated me like trash. *Couldn't you outwit a clod like that?* I asked myself.

I doubted very much that he'd be back. He would have assumed that I'd tell the story to my "fiance" and that someone would be here with me by now. But I wasn't going to chance a trip downstairs to see if the door was still locked. If it was open, it could just stay that way till morning.

I was glad I hadn't let on to Jack. It would have lent strength to his argument that I needed protection, and I wasn't ready to admit that, even to myself.

I wrapped some ice cubes in a towel and lay down on the bed, pressing them against the side of my face. I would stay home from work tomorrow if how I looked made it likely that I would have to answer questions.

The telephone set there beckoning me. Just a few quick spins with my index finger, and I could be listening to Herb's voice. It wouldn't even matter what he said. If I could just hear him I'd feel so much better.

For a few minutes.

And then I'd feel worse.

Aren't you a big girl now?

Chapter Twelve

The house was in a row of duplexes on a quiet, orderly street. Jack cut across the frozen lawn and I followed him, asking, "Is your mom expecting us?"

"Sure." He held the front door for me and the warm smell of Sunday cooking enveloped us. "Up here," he said, leading me up the stairs. "The apartment's on the second floor. She doesn't know we're coming *today*, but I told her I'd bring you to meet her soon."

"Jack! You should have called her to ask if today was all right."

"It'll be all right." He opened the apartment door without knocking and we found his mother sitting in an overstuffed chair, darning socks in front of the TV set, the room darkened by drawn shades. After the brilliant sunlight, I had difficulty adjusting my eyes, and I didn't know how she could darn in that light. She must have done it by feel, since she was watching television at the same time.

"Ma, this is Joan." He propelled me toward her chair. "Remember? The girl I told you about?"

"Yes." She looked away from her program briefly to smile at me and indicate the chair next to hers with a nod of her head. "You sit here."

Jack took my coat and I sat down.

"I'm glad to meet you, Mrs. Kerouac." I didn't extend my hand. She would have had to put down her darning to shake it.

"You call me Gabe," she said. The 'beeg bloo eyes' Jack had described were sparkling.

"That's what all her friends call her," Jack explained. "It's short for Gabrielle. See? She likes you already!" He reassured himself more than me, speaking as though his mother weren't present, but then he turned to her and spoke about me the same way.

"She's a seamstress, Ma. Sews, makes dresses, you know?"

She answered him with a barrage of French only slightly resembling any I remembered from high school. He laughed and translated.

"She says she knows what a seamstress is."

"You like cheeken?" she asked me.

"Oh, yes!"

"Good! You stay for dinner."

Jack stood by her chair overseeing our meeting, looking from one of us to the other, beaming hopefully. Or, perhaps, apprehensively?

"I bought her that TV set," he told me proudly. "With money from my book."

"You go get Ti-Nin," Gabe ordered him. "Tell her *she's* here."

"Ti-Nin!" he exclaimed. "What's she doing here?" Aside to me he said, "That's my sister."

Another stream of French from Gabe, answered by Jack's "aah, oh," made me feel that this was family business. I hoped we hadn't chosen the wrong time for a visit.

"Go now," she insisted, and as soon as he was out of the room she whispered to me, smiling secretively, knowingly.

"He's a good boy."

I smiled back, not knowing what response was expected. My

eyes were becoming accustomed to the dim room, and I saw that the furniture had been arranged for TV viewing. The chairs we sat in, large pieces with faded wine-colored upholstery, were almost directly in front of the matching sofa. Horse hairs protruded here and there, placing the date of their manufacture in the twenties or before. I imagined they had been transported from Quebec to Lowell and finally to New York. Jack's oak roll-top desk was beside the set, but his swivel chair could easily be moved back in line with the others to a comfortable viewing position. A variety of small tables were covered with doilies, knick-knacks, photos, and souvenirs which Gabe must have dusted daily, for everything gleamed, spotlessly clean. This was the room Jack had described as homey and cozy. I found it oppressively crowded and close, but then I remembered Bill had accused me of exaggerating the importance of space.

Jack returned with a pretty brown-haired woman, looking younger than her thirty years. She was thin but her hip structure promised the eventual pear shape of her mother's figure. He introduced her as I extricated myself from the deep comfort of the chair.

"My sister, Caroline. She was putting my nephew down for his nap."

Then to Caroline he said, "This is Joan. She's going to be your sister-in-law."

"Oh really? How nice!" she exclaimed. "When. . ."

"Jack," I broke in, "I never said. . ."

"Never mind!" he cut me off. "You'll see. Next week we'll get the license."

Gabe had gone into the kitchen to put dinner on the table and she called to Caroline to help her. I went in too, to see if I could do something, and Jack followed, not wishing to be left alone. The television continued to blare without an audience.

Caroline removed a yellow table cover, shook it out and folded it. Escaping wafts of oilcloth odor floated in the steamy room, reminding me of upstate farm kitchens. Now Gabe replaced it with a white plastic cloth embossed to look like lace. I helped set the table in the midst of the joshing and jostling and the good-natured insults, all in a language I couldn't understand, of this close, loving family. They had a bond and a humor born of kinship, shared values and shared experiences. My own family, though no less loving, seemed reserved and constrained by comparison.

Dinner was chicken-in-the-pot with vegetables, and it was superbly flavored. An unexpected guest made no difference in the portions served at this table, for Gabe had prepared a prodigious amount.

"So much!" I remarked to Jack.

"She always cooks a lot on Sundays so I'll have something to eat while she's at work." We spoke in English while Gabe and Caroline continued to converse in French.

"Your mom works?" I had thought he supported her.

"Yeah. She's a leather skiver at a shoe factory. She uses a little tool that scrapes the leather and thins the edges so they can be rolled and stitched."

Our conversation turned to other subjects and though we spoke softly, the mention of Allen's name did not escape Gabe's notice.

"You know Geensbairg?" she asked me, almost accusingly.

"Yes," I admitted.

"Communist Jew!" she spat out.

"Now, Ma..." Jack began.

"You know what zay do!" Gabe continued.

"No Ma, please! Not now!" Caroline tried to stop her, but Gabe overruled both of them.

"Put poison een ze water! Een ze reservoir zay put it. Poison!"

"Who?" I asked.

"Communists! Foreigners!" she cried venomously.

I wondered what Gabe's definition of that might be, so I asked her, "What's a foreigner?"

"Don't." Jack shook his head and warned me. "You'll just get her started."

"She's already started," I said. "I want to know what she thinks."

While Jack stared out the window in annoyance and Caroline gazed at the ceiling, Gabe attempted to explain.

"Anybody zat doan have... Eef ze grandparents. . ." She gave up and turned the job over to Jack. "Jackie, *you* tell her!"

"Anybody whose grandparents weren't born in the U.S.A.," he imparted reluctantly.

"Ou Canada!" she prompted.

"Or Canada," he obliged.

Gabe nodded her head in satisfaction and Caroline availed herself of the opportunity to change the subject.

"Does your family live in New York, Joan?"

"They live upstate," I told her. "In a small town near Albany. But we're from Forest Hills, originally. I was born in the Jamaica Hospital, as a matter of fact."

"Oh! That's quite close to here. You must feel right at home."

"I was very young when we left. We moved to California during the Depression, so I don't remember anything about Forest Hills."

"I remember the Depression very well," Caroline said. "How old are you now?"

When I answered that I was twenty, Gabe clucked her disapproval.

"Too young!" she objected. "Too young to be away from ze mother!"

"Oh, Ma," Caroline sighed, "lots of girls live alone nowadays."

"It's all right," Jack said. "She won't be alone much longer."

It was my turn to change the direction of the conversation. "How old is your little boy, Caroline?"

"Little Paul is two," she said. "He's named after his father."

"And you live in South Carolina?"

"In North Carolina. We came up by train last night and Little Paul hardly slept. He'll have a good long nap." She got up to clear the table while Gabe served us warm apple pie and coffee.

"Joan says she can't make a good pie crust, Ma," Jack told his mother as she and Caroline sat down.

"Ees no very hard," Gabe said to me. "I show you."

"I knew she'd say that!" Jack laughed.

"I'd love to be able to make a pie like this, Gabe," I told her. "This is delicious!"

"I make for Jackie, apple. He like eet best."

"But you should taste her *cherry* pie, Joan," Caroline said. "Ma makes the best—" She rolled her eyes as she was interrupted by a call from her son.

"What happened to that long nap?" Jack asked.

"Oh, well," she said, getting up, "I guess it was just wishful thinking." Jack followed her to the bedroom and Gabe and I did the dishes.

"Why you come to New York?" Gabe asked me.

"There are better jobs here," I evaded.

"Ah yes, but to leeve alone! Ees no good!"

"I've been looking for a roommate."

"Much better you have husband. One girl, two girl, no make deeference. Ees no safe!"

I busied myself looking for a cupboard for the glasses, not willing to say it aloud, but ready to agree with her.

"Thees one." Gabe opened the cupboard over the sink. "I tell you, Jeanne," she said, converting my name to the French, "Jackie bee good husband. He love ze cheeldren and no chase ze girls. Some day he make good money. You see. He's a good boy and you're a good girl. I like to have you my daughter."

"Thank you, Gabe." I didn't take this compliment lightly, after all I'd heard about her rejection of Jack's friends.

Jack came into the kitchen with a sunny-faced little boy in tow. His blond hair fell down over his brow and his blue eyes were the duplicate of his grandmother's.

"Give Memere a kiss," Jack said.

"Mere kiss!" he cried happily and ran to her. She dried her hands and gathered him up in her arms, kissing his round little cheek and speaking to him in French.

"French will only confuse him, Ma," Caroline cautioned. "We want him to learn English first."

Gabe put him down, saying something to the effect that she never thought she'd see the day when a grandchild of hers would not speak French.

"It will be easier for him when he goes to school," Jack agreed. He would know. He had told me how difficult it had been to have to learn to read and write in a language he could barely understand.

"Let's take Little Paul out to the park," Jack said to me. He turned to his sister. "Okay, Nin? Can we do that?"

"If you don't keep him out too long," she answered. "He's not used to the cold."

"Dress him warm," Jack advised her. "And we'll take his ball. If he's active he won't be cold." He went with Caroline to help dress Little Paul.

As I got my coat from the hall closet I heard her say to him, "Don't you dare go off and get married and leave Ma alone again, Jack! She'll come and stay with us, and believe me, our marriage is too shaky right now to survive that kind of strain."

"Aw, don't worry about it." Jack replied. "Ma wants me to get married anyway."

He came out carrying his nephew on his shoulders, ducking under the doorway. "This is Joan, Ti-Paul. Can you say 'Aunt Joan?'"

"Antome," Paul obliged.

"Hey! That's pretty good," Jack said. "He calls me 'Untadat.'"

We made our way downstairs slowly, Jack ducking where necessary, and once outside, Paul cried "Horsie! Horsie!" Jack complied by breaking into a trot and giving a convincing whinny.

"Hey, don't pull my hair, you little bugger!" He put up his hands for Paul to use as reins, and slowed down to a walk.

"Listen," he said to me. "Don't pay any attention to my mom when she gets going like she did about the Jews. She's just very narrow-minded on this score. Always has been. Best thing is not to let her get started."

"It's not her fault," I said. "Hasn't her exposure to the world been pretty limited?"

"Well, I don't know. She's been working for years. It isn't as if she's been sheltered or isolated."

"But who does she work with? Not Jews, I bet!"

"No," he chuckled. "A Jew owns the factory. That only adds to the prejudice she already had. The women she works with are mostly Italian, Irish, and Spanish, with a few scattered Poles and French. And just about all Catholic, I guess."

"And they probably share her view of the world. You would too, if you hadn't gotten out of Lowell and gone to school. If you hadn't examined the world for yourself, you'd have nothing to counteract her prejudice with."

"Yeah? Maybe."

"I think you should bring more people home, and take her to

town with you once in a while. Give her a chance to see what the world is like outside the shoe factory. *She's* the one who's being short-changed."

"Nah, nah. You don't know her. She doesn't even like half the people she works with. They're 'foreigners.' And in Lowell we lived among Greeks and she didn't like them. She's hopeless. But she's very good and sweet in her own way. In her own innocent, ignorant way."

"Horsie! Horsie!" Paul was impatient with our talk. Jack gave a little jump to make him laugh.

"Anyway, I'm glad you don't hold her narrow-mindedness against her," Jack concluded, as he trotted into the park and deposited the little boy on a huge flat rock. The sun was bright and the rock was warm in spite of the chilly air. I sat on it and watched them play with the ball till Jack threw it across the field and asked Paul to get it.

"He's the one who needs the activity," Jack said, sitting down beside me. "Not me."

But Paul, seeing us sitting idly, abandoned the ball and ran back to climb up onto the rock and join us.

"Where ball?" Jack asked him. "Paul get ball. Give to Jack."

Paul looked at Jack and laughed.

"Why do you talk to him that way?" I asked. "You're teaching him baby talk."

"But he *is* a baby. Gotta keep it simple."

"If you don't want him to wait for school to learn English, why should he have to wait till then to know how sentences are constructed?"

"But that's too much to expect of a little kid," Jack objected.

"Too much to say, maybe, but not too much to understand. Look." I put my arm around Little Paul. "Paul, will you please get the ball and bring it to me?" He jumped down, ran to get the ball, and ran back to place it in my lap. "Thank you, Little Paul." I lifted him onto my lap and hugged him. "Thank you for not proving me wrong."

"Well, how do you like that!" Jack said. "Where'd you learn so much about kids?"

I smiled. "I spent half my childhood baby-sitting. And I was a kid myself. Don't you remember listening to adults make fools of themselves talking down to you?"

"No, I don't remember anything like that, but maybe that's because of the language difference. When I was little my mom spoke even less English than she does now. So her attempts to teach me were pretty simple." He stood up and bounced the ball absently, looking at me shyly, like a schoolboy. I was seeing the Jack I liked best today, straight and sober, showing no trace of the gloom he often conveyed, and exhibiting none of the irritability and false confidence I found annoying. "I want to have eight kids like Old Man Martin in my book," he said, throwing the ball into the air. "There's no nicer sound than the sound of kids yelling and playing in the yard. And when I'm old I'll put my feet up on the oven door of the wood stove and listen to my grown children tell me about the world as they see it."

Little Paul was pulling at Jack to get him to come and play.

"And in the evening of our life together, you'll read stories to our grandchildren," he finished, and then he gave his attention to his nephew.

"Okay, Ti-Paul. What do you want to do?"

"Run!" Paul shouted and took off across the park. The little boy had no fear of falling. He bounced along unsteadily but weightlessly, and Jack followed close behind, pretending he was having difficulty keeping up, allowing Paul to stay just out of reach. Paul laughed happily as he ran and screamed excitedly when Jack reached out to almost tag him. Finally Jack caught him up and swung him around. The laughter of the man and the boy reached me from across the park and made an imprint upon some blank unfulfilled space within me, and I heard myself thinking *that's what I want.* But at the same time I suspected that I was a victim of subliminal advertising.

Was it so simple? Just to put away doubts and take the necessary practical steps to make the farmhouse and the children a reality? Was that all there was to it? Maybe I was beginning to abandon a vision, paring down the dream to a realizable, manageable size.

Between us there was not even a physical attraction we might have mistaken for love or magic. We would never share the miracle of a sunrise while singing silent hymns of praise. Nor would we know the solemn commitment of standing hand in hand in the Fifth Avenue Presbyterian Church, listening to Handel's Messiah. There was no weakness in the knees, no trembling, no sigh, none of the catching in the throat I had felt with Herb. That magic was memory. I knew better than to make any attempt to duplicate it. If one like that succeeded, it would result in pain, need, and subjectivity. If it failed, there would only be subsequent attempts, a jaded appetite, a blasphemy of the memory itself.

I was a candidate for a hermitage, except for my determination to have children. I could almost see my children now, before they were born, especially the daughter who would be first, who had spoken to me in a dream, and I anticipated her birth as the manifestation of an idea. Not just mine, but the largest idea, one that predated all life.

For me, Jack's appeal lay more in what he was not than in what he was. He was not sexually aggressive, not intellectually curious concerning me, not anxious for me to achieve goals or improve myself, and he was neither critical nor demanding except in regard to domestic matters.

I was being wooed because our meeting coincided with Jack's decision to marry, because Bill, before his death, had expected our relationship to be propitious, and because I was acceptable to his mother. It helped that I could cook and that I was no threat to him, would not upstage him. And it was convenient that we shared a dream of children. His reasons may have been more complicated, and his feelings may have been deeper, but this was all I saw, all I wanted to see.

My view of the situation was that we could be, for each other, a means to an end. On this bright November day, it seemed suddenly a workable solution to a number of problems. It was the least of a number of evils.

Chapter Thirteen

On Tuesday, November 14, we went to city hall to get the license, and Jack found he was missing some important papers concerning the annulment of his first marriage to Frankie Edith Parker. He called the attorney who had handled the case, and then had to wait for a return call to confirm the fact that her father had indeed had the marriage annulled. The clerk's office stayed open thirty-four minutes beyond closing time to accommodate us.

So on Friday, November 17th, we were about a half hour short of the required seventy-two hour waiting period, and city hall was closing for the weekend. Jack was furious.

"Do you mean you can't stay open another thirty-four minutes?" he asked the clerk.

"The judges have all gone home," she explained. Jack walked ahead of me down the stairs, pouting.

"We can get married on Monday, Jack." I tried to be helpful.

"But the reception's tonight! You don't have a wedding *after* a reception. And there's the beer keg waiting. And all those people! Why does everything have to go wrong?" I smiled, amused at his outburst, as he threw his cigarette butt into the gutter angrily and scowled at me as though it were my fault. "And you *laugh*!" he shouted. "Why are you laughing?"

I composed myself and made a suggestion. "Why don't we just go back and *tell* them we got married? Then the beer can be drunk and everybody will be happy."

"You're not serious!" he said.

"I'm not? Okay, what'll we do?" We walked aimlessly, but in a general uptown direction, and I realized I had forgotten to get my new shoes. Just as well. These were comfortable, even if they didn't match my suit.

"I got it!" Jack spun around. "We can go to a judge I know. Come on!" We ran to a subway entrance and in a few minutes we had reached the Village, and were running up the exit stairs. "I'll just make a phone call and we'll be all set," he said, still running and steering me toward a Walgreen's. Once inside I stopped at a greeting card display and let him sprint ahead to the phones while I put on a browsing attitude and caught my breath.

Jack pulled the door to the phone booth closed, then opened it to look around for me.

"Come over here!" he ordered loudly, when he had located me. I bristled at his dictatorial tone, and took my time getting there.

"Now don't go away!" he said irritably.

"Did you think I was trying to escape?"

"Shhh!" He was dialing.

Arrangements made, we went to Horatio Street to be married by Judge Vincent Lupiano, a relative of Jack's by marriage.

"Do you want hearts and flowers?" he asked. "Or shall we just get it over with?"

"Any way you want to do it will be all right, Judge." Jack was easy to please now that his objective was in sight. The judge called in his wife and secretary as witnesses, and we got it over with. Jack's mother's ring, blessed by the Pope, was on my finger, and the judge poured each of us a shot. After the marriage certificate was signed, Jack took my arm and prepared to leave.

"Thanks a lot, Judge," he said.

"I'm still waiting for you to kiss your bride, Jack," the judge remarked.

"Oh yeah. That's right." He kissed me perfunctorily and said, "Now *that's* taken care of."

In the hallway I told him, "I'd like to get my shoes on the way back."

"Sure!" He was all smiles now. "There's a Thom McCan's just a coupla blocks from here."

* * *

The reception was well underway when we arrived. Some two hundred people were packed into the loft, and they hadn't found it necessary to wait for us in order to celebrate. Nobody even noticed our arrival till we got to the kitchen. Lucien Carr, Allen Ginsberg, Bill Frankel, and John Holmes were in there by the beer keg. Holmes introduced me to his wife, Marian, a vivaciously attractive girl with straight honey-colored hair and a scintillating smile full of perfect white teeth. We all piled into the breakfast nook where Jack and I, conspicuous in our sobriety, received best wishes and congratulations, delivered in varying degrees of sincerity. Marian stretched full length across three of our laps to give Jack an elaborate wedding kiss, and Holmes presented us with a bottle of champagne, saying, "I believe in you, Jack and Joan. I believe in you."

Perhaps he felt we needed the support. We had so little understanding of the action we had just taken. Jack and I knew individually what we were doing but we had not discussed our motives, even with each other. The one concession I had asked of him was that he refrain from the meaningless declarations of love he thought were expected.

His requests of me had not been verbalized, but I knew even from the few days I had known him that he wanted me to listen to everything he had to say, without contribution or criticism. Beyond this we were playing it by ear. We had made a commitment to the marriage, but none to each other.

Halfway through his first drink Jack began to mimic the drunken state he aspired to. He assumed an expression of innocent glazed-eyed surprise with eyebrows raised and one finger in the air to command attention. His look said, "But wait!.," as though he were performing a magic trick. I had witnessed this transformation of speech and gesture after as few as three swigs of beer, and would have believed he was actually drunk if I hadn't been monitoring his consumption. It was not an act—it was more like a conditioned response.

I wandered around the loft to see who was there that I knew. Our reception was typical of a well-advertised party, in that most of those present were uninvited. An unsmiling studious-looking girl intercepted me, possibly because of my corsage, to ask "Where is the bride?"

"Right here," I said.

"Oh dear!" Her eyes took in my conservative pin-checked suit. "I was expecting something more festive!"

There were wedding gifts to be unwrapped and more friends of Jack's to meet. It hadn't occurred to me to invite Sarah or anyone else I knew. The whole thing had been Jack's idea, and I had seen it as his party, and his wedding for that matter, and let him plan it. None of it seemed to have anything to do with the rest of my life. I felt that I had walked onto a stage set, and I half-expected to walk behind the beer keg and find that it was just a prop, real only from the vantage point of the audience. The room was full of extras I had never seen before, and in a short while they would leave the set and the main characters would resume their real identities.

It finally came to an end early Saturday morning. The last guests found their way noisily down the stairs and I was left with the star of the show. He sat on the bed, raving to himself, falling over from time to time and then righting himself.

"Donsha wanna wear diaphanous gowns?" he inquired, no longer focusing. He raised one finger in the air to explain, "'S. . .," and then forgot what he was explaining.

"I know," I told him. "It's W.C. Fields."

"'S right!" he said, hiccuping. "'S doubla see feels. Wesher nightie?"

"I'll show you my nightie when you show me your pajamas."

"Sin err." He waved an arm in the direction of his suitcase. I got them out and threw them to him. He smiled vacantly at his pajama top as he held it up for my inspection and then fell over on it.

"No you don't!" I shook him. "Get your pajamas on! I'll get your shoes off. You do the rest." I pulled off his shoes and went into the kitchen to put away the perishables. Hearing no sound from Jack, I called to him.

"Jack! Are you getting your pajamas on?"

"Uh," was the answer I got.

I found that he had taken his clothes off, at least. That was a good start. "Come on, Jack." I helped him. "First this arm. Then this leg. Now under the covers with you!"

"Wesher nightie?"

"I'm getting it on now." I turned out the bedside lamp on my way to the bathroom and put on the "diaphanous gown" Jack had insisted I buy for the occasion. By the time I got into bed he was completely out. So far, the marriage had lived up to my expectations.

* * *

Daylight revealed muddy tracks from one end of the loft to the other. Hundreds of feet had walked through the beer from the dripping spigot. I got into my jeans and hung the fragile nightgown on the hook in the bathroom.

The kitchen had gotten the worst of it. I'd start there while the coffee perked. I filled a basin with suds and began sponging at one end of the room.

"Hey! What are you doing up so early?" Jack called from the bed. "Come back here!"

"Not till I get this floor washed."

"Floor washed? You have to wash the floor the morning after our wedding?"

"You should see it!" I said.

He got up, put on a plaid bathrobe and stood at the edge of the tiled floor.

"The black ones don't look too bad," he observed. "Just the white ones."

"Why don't you wash the black ones then, and I'll wash the white ones?"

"You can't be serious! I haven't even had my coffee!"

"After the floor," I said mercilessly.

"Then will you come back to bed? I didn't even see you in your nightgown last night. Too dark. Can we have our coffee in bed?"

"Sure."

"All right. Give me the other sponge. I'll start at this end."

I poured some suds into another pan and set it with the sponge at his end of the kitchen. We squatted opposite each other, working our way toward the middle.

"Jack! Your tail's in the water!" I laughed as he extracted his bathrobe tie from the suds and held up its dripping tassel, regarding it sadly.

"This is a terrible way to start married life," he said.

"It is?"

"How are you feeling this morning, anyway?"

"What do you mean?"

"Well, last night... I mean, it was our wedding night. Was I... Was everything all right?" He looked at me shyly and then applied the sponge to the floor industriously. I scrutinized his face.

"Jack, I don't know how to say this, but you're. . ." It was my turn to look down at the floor in embarrassment. "Well ... you're everything I could have wanted in a husband."

"Yeah? Let's get finished here and get back to bed. You'll put that pretty nightie back on?"

"Of course."

"You'll probably have to do this side over later." He was losing his balance, slipping and sliding around on the wet floor. Finally he reached the middle. "How's that coffee? Boy, I must have tied one on last night. What a head I've got!"

I tiptoed across the floor to get the coffee pot, and he got back under the covers with a groan. I brought our coffee to the bedside table and sat down.

"Thought you were going to put on your nightie," he reminded me.

"I don't want my coffee to get cold."

"It won't. Hurry so you'll be right back."

After a couple of sips, I went back to the bathroom to change. Approaching the bed, I was conscious of Jack's appraisal. There was something humiliating about being looked at like that, being judged like a horse. *Was I high in the withers? How were my flanks?* Oh well, I had brought it on myself. I walked awkwardly to minimize the effect of the nightgown and got into bed.

"Ah, lovely, lovely. Now you look like a bride."

"I should have worn it at the reception."

There was laughter in the hall as feet tramped up the stairs and fists pounded on the door.

"All right, you lovers! You've been in bed long enough!" It was Lucien's voice.

"Aw, wouldn't you know!" Jack said, getting up. "Why does everything have to go wrong?" He opened the door to admit Lucien and Allen.

"Rise and shine!" Allen said. "We came to help you drink that other bottle of champagne."

"Throw me my robe, will you, Jack?" I asked.

He brought it to me and apologized, "Sorry. We'll get back to this later."

While they popped the cork in the kitchen, I changed in the bathroom for what I hoped would be the last time, and I wondered how far I should go in dispelling Jack's fear that he might disappoint or deprive me. So far there was nothing in the marriage that could be destroyed by the knowledge that I was as uninterested as he was. But I couldn't predict his reaction, didn't know how it would affect the future. The wall was nothing more than a sheet of fiberboard, and I could hear Jack saying,

"Man, we wailed all night! Sweetest little girl in the world!"

"And the floor's clean!" Allen said. "What did you do, Jack? Make her wash the floor before she went to bed?"

"Ah, she's a real woman. I tell you, that little girl can do anything!"

I joined them and poured myself a glass of champagne, and I spoke to Allen. "Remember what Celine said? 'All women are housemaids at heart.'"

"Now!" said Jack. "The next order of business is to get my desk moved in here."

Chapter Fourteen

Before the day was over Jack had prevailed upon some friends, found a truck and moved the desk in. It was deposited near the door in the front of the loft, and we debated its permanent location.

"Why don't we put it right here in front, by the window?" I suggested. "This area was intended to be the studio anyway." It seemed logical that Jack's writing place should be separate from what he considered my province, the kitchen, and separate from what constituted the bedroom, right next to the kitchen. I liked the fact that two people could live in this place without getting in each other's way.

"I'd like it closer to the kitchen," Jack said. "It feels too far from the 'home fires' out here."

"You don't want to move the bed, do you?" I didn't want the furniture rearranged.

"Would that be sacrilegious? Just because the bed's always been there, does that mean it has to stay there?"

"It's here because this is the best place for it," I said stubbornly, standing in front of it.

"Well," he considered, "I want the desk right next to the bed then. I have to be in a little corner somewhere, sort of enclosed. If

138

there were room in the kitchen, I'd put it there."

I gave in, not very graciously, and took one end of the desk so we could set it in place, under Cezanne's Mardi Gras. The combination struck me as incongruous and I asked Jack, "How do you feel about that painting? Maybe the desk should really be somewhere else."

"It's all right," he said. "It can stay there."

The typewriter was placed on the desk and Jack put on his sheepskin slippers and sat down, getting the feel of the new location.

"I think I can write here. Coffee!" he demanded in jest, one finger in the air. "Yeah. It'll be alright."

Later, while I was busy in the kitchen, Jack called to me from his desk.

"I want to talk to you. Come and sit down."

"Can't you talk to me from there? I'm making a salad."

"No. I don't feel that I have your attention, and this is important."

I washed the onion off my hands and took the towel with me, drying my hands as I sat on the bed.

"Now look. This is something I've been meaning to talk to you about. It's your attitude toward this place. You don't want a nail driven in any of these walls. Everything has to stay the same. You have to finish every little odd job, just the way Cannastra wanted it done. Doesn't that sound like you're making a shrine of the place?"

"No." I refused to see what he was driving at.

"Well, it does to me. Remember what you said about his funeral? That you didn't want to go and look at his empty body because he wasn't there?"

"Yes," I said.

"Where did you think he was? Here? This place is the same

thing. It's his empty house. He's not here any more, and he does-
n't need this place any more than he needs his body."

"But what do you do for a friend who dies? I feel the least I can
do is keep the place the way he wanted it. When your father died,
didn't you feel that you should finish what he didn't have time to
do?"

"Sure! Take care of my mom! But that's a living thing. You're
doing a dead thing. The best any of Bill's friends can do in his
memory is to get on with their lives, the way he would have
wanted them to."

I looked around the loft at the bookshelves Bill wouldn't need,
and the windows whose light he had no use for, and I began to
wonder why I hadn't seen this for myself.

"I never thought of it that way before, Jack. I didn't really analyze what I was doing at all." I looked around and saw new potential for all the room in this lovely loft. "I think I've been reacting
absently, sort of waiting to see where circumstances would take
me, waiting for the cards to be dealt."

"Looks like Bill dealt you one card in the form of this loft. We
probably never would have met if you hadn't been living here."

"That's true enough, but it was Fred who dealt the card."

"Fred?" Jack asked.

"Fred Cannastra, Bill's brother. He made the arrangements
with the realtors."

"Yeah? Well, just the same, I bet old Bill is looking down at us
right now and saying, 'So Jack and Joan found each other at last.
It's fitting that it should have happened in my loft.' We could say
that this marriage was made in heaven."

"You don't really believe that, do you, Jack? That Bill's dead
spirit has an individual consciousness and human opinions?"

"Sure!" he answered. "Don't you?"

"No!" I shook my head emphatically. "I think this personal ego thing is only for this life. Before we're born and after we die, we're part of some immense all-encompassing consciousness. Sort of a collective. A universal consciousness, I guess you could call it."

"*You* could call it," Jack said, looking at me strangely. "Look. I don't want to argue with you about this right now. Just promise me one thing. Don't ever talk to my mom that way."

I smiled. "Don't worry. I couldn't." I stood up to go back to the kitchen, feeling better than I had when Jack had called me in. "Thanks for talking to me about the way I was acting, Jack. What you said really made sense."

"I had to tell you that. You made me feel like I was sharing the loft with a ghost. And I want you to know that I *won't* share my wife with one."

"Not a chance!" I said. "I don't believe in ghosts."

"Wish *I* didn't. Well, I'll get back to what I was doing. See what I found in that cabinet over there? This whole big roll of paper the same width as typing paper." He had fed the teletype roll into the typewriter, and the three or four feet he had already typed lay over the roll and hung down behind the desk.

"What are you going to do?" I asked. "Roll it up as you type?"

"Yeah. Every night I'll roll it up. It'll save me the trouble of putting in new paper, and it just about guarantees spontaneity. Go back and finish your salad now, and you might refill my coffee cup when you get a chance." He sat back for a moment, gazing at the Cezanne. What would he see there, I wondered as I walked away? Who would be the harlequin and who the clown?

* * *

I had had the feeling all day that something was missing from the loft, and at dinner I finally put my finger on it. The music was gone. I had been able to hear it in my imagination all the time I had been here alone, but not today. Magic was so very fragile. The mere hint of change could cast it instantly into the stone of memory. How would Jack take it if I told him I had been listening to Bill sing arias from *The Marriage of Figaro*?

"Why so quiet?" Jack asked, shaking grated parmesan onto his spaghetti.

"I was thinking that we need music here. There's no music. Have you noticed that?"

"Should we get a phonograph?"

"I guess we should get busy job hunting first. I wouldn't want to buy a phonograph when we don't even have December's rent put aside." The money I had saved was going fast.

"You're right, but do we have to discuss practical things tonight? We've only been married one day. Don't we deserve a few days of honeymoon?"

"I suppose so, but December's so close. Are you going out tonight?"

"Not tonight. I just want to get used to being here with you, writing here. You know, it's sort of like putting on a new pair of shoes. I have to break this new life in."

"That's an interesting way to put it. I guess I'm doing the same thing. Does it pinch?"

"What?"

"Being married. Does it pinch like a new pair of shoes?"

He didn't answer right away, but moved his spaghetti aside and dumped the contents of his salad bowl onto his dinner plate.

"Don't you like to eat it from the bowl?" I asked.

"I like to mix the flavors while I'm eating. And, you see," he returned to the first question, "I'm not going to let it pinch. Marriage isn't the same for a man as it is for a woman. For a woman it's her whole life, but a man has other things to do. His home and marriage serve as a pivot point."

"I don't know where you get the idea that it's my whole life." I wanted to make it clear to him right away that I saw the marriage as a pivot point for myself as well.

"But it is!" he said dogmatically. "A woman gets her view of the world from the information her husband brings back to her. It's in her own best interest to keep him comfortable and satisfied in the place he emanates from. He goes out into the world and does things in it and brings the results back to her."

"Listen, Jack. Your premise is wrong. You're saying that all women are thus and so, and that since I'm a woman I must be thus and so."

"Yeah. Look!" He took a pen and a piece of paper from his desk and wrote on it:

All A are B

C is A

Therefore C is B

"That's what I just said," I told him. "But. . ."

"That's logic," he said. "And you said you didn't go to school."

"It doesn't take school to see that. But Jack. . ."

"You see? It's only logical. You're a woman and in time you'll be a very good woman." He crumpled up the paper and threw it into the basket.

"But Jack!" I was annoyed. "Not all A are B!"

"Oh well, never mind." He waved away my objection. "New shoes need to be broken in. I'm going to get back to work now. This book is going to be the means of getting that land you want so badly. So when you hear me typing, just think of an old farm house, some chickens and a cow in the San Joaquin Valley, or maybe up in Mendocino County. California is full of beautiful farmland. When we get to San Francisco we'll drive around with Neal and Carolyn and have a good look at it. Then when I sell the book, we'll pick out our spot and settle down."

"And then what?" I asked, clearing the table.

"Then we'll make babies and more books. Oh, I can just picture you looking proudly at our children over your high cheek bones."

I felt my cheek bones. "Are they any higher than most?"

"Yes, go look at them. They're like an Indian's. You're my Apache that I've always dreamed about." He pronounced it "Aposh" and began to sing a French folk song about a boy who falls in love with an Indian maid. I did the dishes, thinking about how we all see what we want to see rather than what's really there. No one had ever told me I had high cheekbones before. I failed to find them in the mirror over the sink.

Jack's plan to spend the evening at home was forgotten when friends arrived, urging him to go out. He didn't wait for taunts about his being tied down by his marriage. He put on his coat and left immediately.

* * *

Jack had put other manuscripts aside to work exclusively on *On The Road*, but he had brought parts of *Dr. Sax* and *Visions of Gerard* with him and needed an out-of-the-way storage spot. There were innumerable nooks and crannies in the loft, and I went out to shop for groceries, leaving him to choose the one best place suited for his purpose.

I returned to find him sitting in bed surrounded by my own familiar pages and manila envelopes. All my life I had spewed out my insane dreams and nightmares. I had always dissected and examined my ideas on paper. Now he sat there with the intimate evidence in his hands, denuding me, intellectually and emotionally. I instantly felt a deep, traumatic sense of violation. He could know me without my consent. He looked up from reading and extended his arm to encompass all the words piled on the bed.

"Yours?" he asked.

The heat of indignation rose in me as I answered.

"Of course they're *mine*." My head filled with rushing sounds, and my nostrils dilated. I could feel angry pain extending from some point inside my skull as if it were a silk thread, across my cheek, down my neck, through my body to my toes. The thin thread stretched tighter, vibrating, cutting into my organs until I thought I would scream, cry, or smash something.

And then, suddenly, the thread snapped. My head cleared and I was detached again, insulated in calm and invulnerability. I shivered in the familiarity of this feeling. It was the complete void of emotions I'd known before I met Herb, before I knew pleasure or pain. And here it was back again, and not unwelcome. I had despaired of finding it again. Would it stay this time? I shook from the exertion of the transition. I felt as if I'd been taken, ground up, and reconstituted.

"They're really pretty good," Jack said, oblivious to the trauma I'd just brought myself through. "But you share a fault with all women. Too sentimental. Mawkish. This one. . ." He held up the pages. "Do you really feel this way about being alone?"

"That's in the third person," I said. I stepped lightly as I took the groceries to the kitchen. The bubble was around me again, and I let it envelop me.

"But it's obviously you," he continued. "You couldn't have written it with such feeling otherwise."

"Then you've answered your question," I said, hanging up my coat. I picked up the stacks one by one, tapped the edges even against the desk, and took them away.

"Don't be so defensive!" he said, laughing. "You should appreciate criticism."

"This wasn't intended for any critic's eyes. I don't write for an audience like you do. I just think on paper. It has about as much literary value as a shopping list."

"Then what are you so uppity about? If it isn't a literary effort, what difference does it make?"

"You were looking at the contents of my mind. Don't you see that it's an invasion of privacy? If I were writing for the public I'd appreciate criticism. But I'm using writing as a way of working out ideas."

"And you don't think your ideas can stand up to scrutiny. Is that it? They won't bear examination?"

"I have no intention of finding out," I told him. "I refuse to submit them for your examination or anyone else's. And you wouldn't be interested anyway." What I refused was the intimacy of sharing. I knew that anyone who understood my thoughts would have no need of them and anyone who didn't understand would reject them.

"Well, do whatever you want," Jack said. "I won't read your stuff anymore, as long as you don't have any high-flown ideas about being a serious writer. I can't stand women who think they can write. It's all just so much sentimental bullshit!"

I put the groceries away, lingering for just a moment over the onions. We had plenty already and I shouldn't have bought more, but they were so beautiful I hadn't been able to resist them. I turned one in my hands till the glistening coppery skin rustled off dryly. Held to the light of the window, its delicate translucence surpassed the ballerina's tulles of Degas' paintbrush. One of the old ones would do for the stew. Later, if Jack went out, I'd look at the new ones some more. Not that he cared what I did with my time, as long as dinner was satisfactory and on time.

I realized that I had all but forgotten my distress over his finding my writings, and then abruptly, my mind was back at Lincoln Hospital again.

I'd been in an accident on the Triboro Bridge. I told the doctor who was preparing to sew me up, "Don't give me anesthetic. I won't need it."

He raised his eyebrows and begun to trim the ragged edges of the wound, expecting me to recant. I heard the scissors and felt their pressure and pull, but no pain.

"She's in shock," the doctor had told the nurse.

In shock? No. This was my natural state. Until much later, when I allowed myself to burst through that insulating barrier for Herb. He could never have known the effort it took or the sacrifice it entailed. He hadn't known how far I had come; he could only see how far I had to go. My all had not been enough.

And then, I'd never been able to return myself to this calm cool detachment. The genie was out of the bottle. The bubble sometimes arrived, as a brief visitor, after bursts of anger, but then it left, unable to compete with the memories, still fresh, of the past year.

This time I would keep it. I whispered it to myself, in a stern, determined murmur. "Stay," I commanded myself.

* * *

The weekend after we were married, Lucien, with Allen and Liz, drove us upstate for a visit with my mother. We stopped in Poughkeepsie on the way, to see Jeanne and Jack Fitzgerald, who had gone to Columbia. Listening to Jack and Fitzgerald scatting the blues together was a high spot of the trip.

We had promised ourselves we'd find jobs as soon as we got back from my mother's. If there had been a honeymoon at all, it was over, and we had one week to come up with the rent.

Jack's friends became accustomed to dropping in at any hour of the night, since he slept by day, and while I deplored his lack of assertiveness, he explained that his friends *were* his book. If not this one, then a book of the future. It was in the interest of writing that he allowed them to use his nights this way. I accepted the view with suspicion.

The situation was not conducive to early morning job hunting. We awoke in the afternoon and by the time we finished the lavish breakfasts that had become our habit, the sun was going down.

This night was an exception and it appeared that we would be alone. I had gone to bed and Jack sat at his desk.

"Will the light bother you?" he asked.

"Not if I turn the other way." I rolled over to face the kitchen.

He typed rapidly for some minutes, then said, "This is the way it should be more often. I like watching you sleep while I work. Dream of me, because I'll be joining you soon."

A voice in the street began to call a familiar name over and over, pleadingly. "Bill, Bill, Bill!" I got up and went to the window.

"What are you doing?" Jack asked. "Get back to bed!"

"I'll do no such thing!" I said, opening the window. It was Bob Steen, weaving and lurching in the street.

"Steen!" I called and threw down the keys. He missed them but found them in the street.

"Now what did you do *that* for?" Jack's annoyance was apparent.

"I can't let him stagger around out there in his delusion."

"Why not?" he asked. "What's he to you?"

"A friend! You know what a friend is, don't you?"

"But you're my wife!" he objected, as if this had anything to do with Steen's problem.

"Would the fact that you're my husband have anything to do with your giving a friend a place to sleep?"

"But my friends are men!"

"By a strange coincidence, most of mine are too," I said. I went out to the hall to see what was taking him so long. He had stopped halfway up to lie down.

"Steen!" I called. "You've got a little farther to go."

He looked in my direction but didn't seem to know where he was any more. "Come on," I urged. "There's something more comfortable to sleep on up here."

He raised himself with an effort and continued upward. I took the keys from his hand as he came inside. Now he knew where he was and headed straight for the bathroom, with Jack's dark inhospitable looks following him. I got out the extra bedding and made a sleeping place in the kitchen on the car seat, placing a chair at one end for his feet. I had slept on the car seat many times when Bill lived here, and Steen probably had as well. I doubted he even knew Jack was there.

"So comfortable," he mumbled. "Didn't know... could be... so comfortable." He pulled the covers up to his chin and was asleep instantly.

Jack stood at his desk, rolling a joint, his back to the kitchen, throwing dagger-like looks over his shoulder in the direction of his unwelcome guest. Nobody could glower as darkly as Jack, but he never acted on his anger, except for an occasional nasty remark. He was finished typing for the night and soon came to bed, turning his back to me without a word. I could only speculate as to the reason for his extreme displeasure at having Steen there. I supposed it was something in the past, just as it must have been something in my own past that wouldn't allow me to leave him outside. I struggled against the urge to remind Jack of the night he and I had met, just a few short weeks ago.

Steen was gone by the time we awoke, but Jack wouldn't stop talking about how the whole night had been ruined by the intrusion.

"We're not going to stay here," he declared. "You can't seem to get these guys off your tail and I'm not going to put up with a steady stream of drunks coming up here to see you."

"*What* guys?" I asked. "If you don't want to count Steen among your friends, then he's the only person exclusively *my* friend to have come up here since we married. And he didn't come to see me anyway. He'd gotten drunk and come looking for Bill, just like he used to do."

We both knew that no amount of drink could have made him forget that Bill was dead, but he had come anyway. We were all coming to grips with the reality of Bill's death and understanding each other's aberrations in this regard was just part of the process.

"He knew!" Jack said. "You can't tell me he didn't know Bill was dead."

"It doesn't make any difference."

Steen's night on the car seat made it easier for Jack to ignore the real reason for the move. We had no way to pay the rent anyway, having lived as though we were independently wealthy. Jack called his mother and told her I had finally agreed to come with him to Richmond Hill, and told me we'd find it easier to save money once we moved in with her.

"Assuming we earn any," I said.

Chapter Fifteen

Gabe's happiness overflowed in unashamed tears as Jack's desk was returned to the spot in the living room where I had first seen it, and she ceremoniously placed his sheepskin slippers beneath it.

"Thanks to God!" she sobbed, hugging both of us. "Eet was so ampty, so lonely." Her relief was a balm for my bitterness about losing the loft, which I supposed was a small deprivation compared to what she must have suffered without her son. But how would she take it when we left for San Francisco? Jack had assured me we'd only be here until we saved enough money for the trip. I hoped he had told his mother.

"Come. I show you. I fix for you bedroom." She led us through Jack's tiny bedroom, unused these past few weeks, and into her large front bedroom.

"Oh, Gabe! Don't give up your room," I objected. "The typewriter will keep you awake all night." Jack's old room was right next to the living room, and was the only access to the front room from the rest of the apartment.

"Eet's okay," she insisted. "I no mind typewriter."

"And the bed is bigger!" Jack added, sitting on it and bouncing up and down. Gabe returned to the living room to supervise the movers.

"It doesn't seem right that your mom should be put out of her room," I told Jack.

"Don't worry about it! She wants to do it. Besides, my bed is too small for two people."

"Ti-Jeanne!" Gabe called to me from the other end of the apartment, using the feminine counterpart of the affectionate "Ti-Jean" she often used for Jack. She would find other names for me later, and I would learn to determine her mood by the name she used. I found her tucking our bedding into the linen closet just outside the bathroom.

"Eet all find place," she said, and taking me by the arm, she bustled me into the living room. "But zees"—she indicated my sewing machine—"we put een hall for now. I show you somesing else." Still gripping my arm, she led me down the hall to a tiny room obviously used for storage. "I ask Jackie take for me zees down to basement. You have room for sew."

"It's wonderful, Gabe!" Like the bedroom, it looked out on the street and the trees, and the best light in the apartment was to be found in these two rooms. "It's just perfect! Thank you so much."

"Ees no too good. Ees no heat, but maybe we find some little heater."

I was mentally transforming the room, making it my own. My worst fear about this move had been that I wouldn't be able to find a corner where I could be by myself.

"We'll find a heater," I told her, "as soon as I find a job."

"Maybe sooner," she said with a smile.

My kitchen utensils formed a merger with Gabe's, and she delighted in examining each addition. She particularly liked a small hand grinder that grated lemon rind, and she inserted a lemon to try it out. Rather than waste the product, we made a batch of lemon cookies on the spot. The aroma drew Jack to the kitchen, where he waited for them to come out of the oven, content for the moment that he had the best of both worlds.

Over a quick supper of cold cuts and potato salad, I told Gabe about our plan to get jobs and save to go to San Francisco. This was not what she had in mind for us.

"You stay home weez husband much better. Make him eat right. How he's gonna write weez no food?" Then she explained to Jack what she wanted us to do, and waited for him to translate.

"She says the neighborhood needs a good dressmaker and *haute couture* designer. If we advertise, you'll be able to stay home and work at the same time."

"I've done that before," I said. "And I know its drawbacks."

"I think it's a good idea. We can give it a try at least."

"Sure we can," I agreed. "If you don't mind wasting a lot of time. In a neighborhood like this, people expect to save money by having things made. Homemade is second best to store-bought. The idea of individuality hasn't occurred to these people because they're still trying to look like everyone else. It'll be another generation before they have any confidence in their own taste."

"What are you saying?" he asked indignantly. "That this is a neighborhood of peasants?"

"That's not what I said. But what I see on the street and through the windows tells me these people aren't interested in being unique. Sears Roebuck is plenty good enough. If you want to equate that with peasantry, go ahead."

He glared at me and sat back in his chair, pouting. "I suppose West 21st Street was a classy neighborhood! You think you've come down in the world by moving in with my mother?"

"I never sewed for people on West 21st Street."

"*Qu'est-ce qu'elle dit* (what's she saying)?" Gabe hung on Jack to know the verdict.

"She says that's a good idea," he lied, to keep the peace.

"I sink you fight," she said to me.

"Oh no, we never fight." I gave Jack a smile only he could interpret.

Gabe beamed her approval and the stage was set for the balance of our stay. Neither of us would cross her.

"You make cards... notes," she said, content now that she was in full control. "Take around. Leave een door. Say 'good sewing,' somesing like zat. You make good money. You see."

"No, Ma! Not like that!" Jack looked at her, aghast. "We have to advertise in the paper, have cards made at the printer's and *mail* them out."

"No, no, no! Take too long. Cost too much. You do my way. You see."

"She's right, Jack." I prolonged the farce. Might as well get some comedy mileage out of it.

Gabe got up to clear the table but I restrained her, having decided the dishes would be my job as long as I was here.

"I'll bring your coffee," I said.

"Such a good girl," Gabe said. "Doan fight weez her, Jackie."

I put the coffee on the table and made a face at Jack when Gabe wasn't looking. In my annoyance with him, I shook more detergent than necessary into the water, and Gabe saw my mountain of suds.

"Too much!" she cried. "Look! Like zees." She shook a small amount into her hand, saying "Enough," and poured it back into the box. "Little sings make beeg difference."

She was right and I nodded in acquiescence, ashamed of my lack of control. Jack smirked as he took his coffee to the living room to watch Sarah Vaughan on the Milton Berle show.

"You learn." Gabe patted my shoulder and followed Jack.

Television was new to me as a way to spend an evening. When the dishes were done, I joined them and watched Gabe darn socks, her eyes never leaving the set.

"Are those Jack's socks?" I asked, hoping darning was not something I was expected to learn.

"Oh, no. For me," she said. "Een my boots nobody see."

All I had ever seen her wear was a faded floral print housedress and bedroom slippers, and I wondered what she would wear with her boots to the shoe factory. I watched a succession of singers, dancers, and comedians, and finally decided to go to bed, feeling logy and dull-headed. How would Jack be able to write with the TV set in the same room?

* * *

In the morning, I was awakened by drops of water in my face. I opened my eyes to Gabe's ample aproned front, leaning across me. She held a glass of orange juice, from which the drops fell.

"Ti-Jean!" She shook him.

"All right, Ma. Thanks." He gulped it down while she waited, and handed back the empty glass. Probably this ritual had taken place every morning of his life that he had awakened at home, and my presence was no obstacle. He had not been so pampered in the two weeks we had been at the loft.

I got up, leaving Jack to sleep the day away, and found Gabe about to go out the door. Dressed in her neat town coat and a little feathered hat, she looked very nice, and I told her so.

"Ti-Jeanne, doan listen to Jackie. He ees *fou*, a stupid boy! You make him type zees paper for give around neighborhood." She tapped the pile of paper she had left on the table.

"All right, Gabe." I assumed they had argued about it after I had gone to bed. "Would you like me to start something for dinner before you get home?"

"Ah, yes. You shop zen." She reached into her bag and gave me a five-dollar bill. "Get somesing nice. But doan listen to Jackie!"

From the doorway she added, "And make him take zose sings in room for sew down to basement."

"Yes, Gabe. I will," I promised. She closed the door and went out into the chill morning. I watched through the little dime-store figurines on the kitchen window sill, and saw her hurrying, duck-like, toward Jamaica Avenue. Sitting with my coffee, I considered the pile of paper. I'd do as she asked because I was in her house and didn't want to offend her. And because I didn't anticipate results anyway. Jack would comply because he was in her debt. She made him so dependently comfortable, he'd never be satisfied anywhere else. I thought of her alternate spoiling and nagging, and wondered if she secretly hoped to keep him from going across the country again.

How strange to be here, coincidentally so close to the Forest Hills homes that had been my grandparents' and my great-grand-parents', and the tennis courts where my mother had played. I felt that I had abdicated responsibility for my own destiny, and at that moment I didn't even care. It was all someone else's show and I was just playing a part in it.

The best part of the day would be making the sewing room my own, but I suspected it would be a long time before Jack got up. I went down the hall and proceeded to empty the room of its con-tents, carrying all the boxes, suitcases, and odds and ends of fur-niture into the living room. I could justify the action by explain-ing that this put the stuff closer to the head of the stairs and therefore closer to its destination. Besides, how was I to clean the room when it was so full?

Wonderful! The living room was now sufficiently congested to preclude normal activity. I almost laughed, imagining Jack's reac-tion. He wanted me to be a stay-at-home dressmaker, did he? At least I'd get my sewing room as a result. After I had scrubbed the little room from top to bottom and moved my sewing machine in,

I soaked in the tub, luxuriating in bath oils. This was a bonus. There had been only a shower at the loft. But there had been space, and I would miss that as much as Jack had missed the cozy womb-like atmosphere of this place.

It was noon, and Jack still slept. We'd never get anything done at this rate. I went into the bedroom and pulled the covers off him.

"Leave me alone!" he yelled. "I didn't go to sleep until three."

"How much sleep do you need? It's noon already!"

"Is it that late?" He sat up. "How long have you been up?"

"Since your orange juice."

He looked embarrassed but didn't comment.

"What's for breakfast?" He yawned his way to the bathroom.

"Will toast and coffee take care of you?" I asked. "Or do you need a production? Your mom wants a few things done today."

"What kind of things?" he called.

"You'll see." I put the bread in the toaster.

At the table he said, "Boy, those breakfasts we had at the loft were great! Now I'm reduced to toast and coffee."

"It'll keep you going for a while and we can have something else later, if you want, but I'm afraid we won't get everything done if we linger over breakfast."

"What's this here for?" He tapped on the pile of paper.

"That's job number two. You're to type up announcements of my arrival so all your lucky neighbors can have custom-designed clothes."

"Aagh, that's really a tacky way to do it."

"The whole thing is tacky. But we'll do it, won't we?"

"Yeah," he sighed. "What's the first job?"

I buffered it, offering him jam for his toast. "It's in the living room."

He turned to look in through the doorway. "Oh Jeez!" he

moaned. "I wish we'd never moved in."

"Too late now..."

"I have to go through the landlady's apartment to get to the basement and I don't even know if she's home."

"Why don't you run down and see?"

"Yeah," he said without enthusiasm, and went downstairs. I had a momentary vision that we would have to put all those things back where they had come from, but all was well. Jack shrugged in resignation, picked up a lamp and a suitcase, and started slowly toward the stairs.

"I'll help you, if you get a move on." I grabbed another suitcase and a box. "But I still have to shop for dinner. Your mom left me the money."

He looked around at me. "How much did she give you?"

"Five dollars, but she didn't say to spend it all, and she told me not to listen to you."

"What is this? A conspiracy against me? Two women! Wow! I didn't know what I was getting into."

The job was done in no time, and while Jack typed up the flyers, four at a time with carbons, I checked out the contents of the pantry so I wouldn't duplicate anything in shopping. By the time we left the house I had a pretty good idea of what we were having for dinner.

As we walked into the butcher's, Jack said "There'll be enough for some beer. Ma won't mind. She always gets me some beer."

"*You* ask her about the beer," I said. "I'm not going to take that responsibility."

"Look in there at that eye round roast!" Jack pointed into the case, giving up the beer as a lost cause.

"We can't do that. She won't like it if we spend it all on meat."

"What else do we need? There are potatoes at home. Come on. Get the roast. She won't care."

"She told me not to listen to you, Jack. When she asks you to shop you can decide."

Jack spun around and went to the window, where he stood looking out, sullen and pouting. A middle-aged woman said to him, "Listen to your sister. She's right. You mustn't make your mother mad."

I giggled.

"My sister! Hah!" Jack stalked outside to wait for me on the sidewalk. As I smiled, I wondered if we might consider the woman's remark prophetic. We had lived with Gabe for only twenty-four hours, and already we were the children in the household. If this continued, we'd be demanding equal portions and tattling on each other.

Gabe was pleased with our performance and liked the pineapple upside-down cake I made. She insisted upon doing the dishes and told us there'd be no television until we had delivered our messages. We ran out to do as we were told, cutting across snow-filled yards, tiptoeing onto porches, hoping no one would see us.

"Stupid, stupid idea," Jack muttered. "I feel like an ass."

"Pretend we were hired to distribute these things," I suggested. "It has nothing to do with us."

"But unfortunately, it has. You know, it's not that I don't have the guts to tell her off, tell her the idea stinks and I won't do it."

"I know, Jack."

"Do you know that I can't hurt her? She's stood by me when no one else would. She's taken more crap from me than anyone should have to put up with, and still she believes in me. Her son wrote a book and he's going to write another one. She thinks I'm some kind of a genius, for krissake."

"Have you read the book to her?"

"Oh yeah. Selected passages, of course. Jeez." He shook his head. "She thinks it's a religious novel." He turned a corner and led me down an alley to a row of trash cans. Lifting a lid, he dropped the rest of his papers in and invited me to do the same.

"Now what'll we do?" I asked. "It's too early to go back."

"There's a little bar a few blocks down this way. I like to watch the types that hang out there."

The appearance of the bar delighted me. Built at the turn of the century, it had resisted the chrome of thirties modernism and the current craze for plastics. Its long curved wooden bar reeked pleasantly of half a century of absorbed alcohol, and the small paned mirrors behind it reflected the nut-colored heavy wood paneling on the opposite wall where the pool table stood.

"I like it," I told Jack as we took stools at the bar.

"Want a beer?" he asked.

"I don't like beer. Sauterne if they have it. Sherry if they haven't."

"You'll have to cultivate a taste for beer. Wine is too expensive."

"But I'm only having one glass. It evens out."

He took a bill from his pocket to pay the bartender, and I remembered that he'd been pleading poverty. "If you had money, why didn't you buy your beer this afternoon instead of trying to wheedle it out of the grocery money?"

"Oh, I'm not above holding out," he admitted.

"I wonder about you. All that talk about how much your mother's done for you, all the crap she's put up with, and yet you don't even try to carry your own weight."

"It's her feelings I'm concerned about. Not her pocketbook. Don't you see the difference?" He looked glum when I didn't answer. "Nah, it's not something you could understand." After a few minutes he got up and went to the back of the bar. I watched the clientele reflected in the mirror, mostly hard hat construction and dock workers. A nice looking man, a little older than Jack, took the stool next to me.

"Are you new in the neighborhood?" he asked pleasantly. "Haven't seen you in here before."

"Yes. My husband and I just moved here yesterday."

"Oh. Welcome to Richmond Hill!" He turned his gaze to the mirror and made no further attempt at conversation. Another man approached the seat Jack had vacated.

"Can I buy you a drink?" he asked.

"No, thank you," I said, pulling the stool closer to mine. "Excuse me but my husband's sitting here."

"He is?" He waved his hand over the stool with a laugh. "Have you got an invisible husband?" I laughed too, and looked around to see where Jack was.

"There he is by the pool table," I said.

Jack was talking to someone but looking at me. He strode to the bar, chug-a-lugged his beer and grabbed my arm, snapping, "Let's get out of here!"

Outside, he asked, "Can't I leave you alone for five minutes without you making eyes at every man in the bar?"

"You're being ridiculous!" I told him. "Want a rundown on the conversation?"

"I don't need one. I saw you laughing with that guy. A perfect stranger! You've got to learn to tell guys like that to fuck off."

* * *

Gabe sat in front of the television set in the dark room and Jack threw off his coat and sat down next to her. I said good- night and went to bed. Any discussion with Jack would be futile. At first I was incensed at being unjustly accused, but the more I thought about it, the clearer it became that Jack believed his interpretation of what he saw, and that this was not so much jealousy as it was a fear that his manhood had been doubted, or at least not taken seriously. To Jack I was a possession. I enhanced his worth, in much the same way a new sled or a BB gun might have when he was a child. If he lacked confidence in his ability to make use of this possession, he imagined that it was coveted, that he was not considered worthy of having it, and that he might lose it to someone who could make better use of it. The boasting to Lucien and Allen the morning after our wedding had been practice for the braggadocio that was to come. Perhaps the fact that not one of Jack's friends could claim any intimate knowledge of me had enhanced my appeal in his eyes. I was an unknown quantity, of unknown quality, and Jack's boasts could not be disputed unless... unless Steen. Steen had heard them.

And Steen had known that the inadequacy was on my part.

* * *

I awoke to the sound of Jack's pained "Ooh! Ouch! Aaaghi*eee*! Son of a *bitch*!" The door flew open as Gabe ran in to investigate. I assumed that he had stubbed his toe as he was always doing, but in the light from the open door I saw him doubled up, naked, clutching his balls.

"Ti-Jean! *Qu'est-ce que passe-t'il* (what happened)?"

"Oh, Jeez! Close the door, Ma, for krissake." He tried to hide behind it from her inquisitive gaze, but she opened it wider and came into the room.

"What happened?" I asked.

He pointed to the wooden footboard and climbed into bed to find privacy under the covers.

"G'wan Ma! Close the door, will you!?"

"Aah! What a clumsy boy!" she said and closed the door.

"I'm so sorry, Jack." I put my hand over the injury to soothe it.

"You should be," he said under his breath. "You did it!"

"*I* did it? You said it was the footboard."

"I wasn't going to tell *her* you kicked me in the balls."

"How could I have? I was asleep!"

"I was trying to get into you without waking you, and you kicked me."

"Oh, no," I said. "You should have waked me. I don't know what I'm doing when I'm asleep. I was dreaming."

"You must have dreamed you were being raped. And your dream would have come true if you hadn't half-killed me."

"Don't try that again. You have to wake me first."

"Get your hand off me. I can't get it up again tonight. It hurts too much."

I turned my back to him and yanked at the covers. "I wasn't exactly lying here waiting and hoping!"

"You never are. I don't think you even like it. Give me back *some* of the covers." He yanked in his direction, untucking them on my side, and I pulled twice as hard, uncovering him.

"Damn it! Knock it off!" he said.

"What will you do if I don't? Tell your ma?"

"Shut the hell up before you make me mad."

Chapter Sixteen

I learned to wake when Gabe's alarm went off. Several times I offered to take the juice in to Jack, but she insisted upon doing it herself. In the same way, she'd give me grocery money, but warn me not to let Jack wheedle his beer out of it. "Doan listen to Jackie! He ees *fou*! A stupid boy!"

But she really believed he was a genius and his every whim should be catered to, and she brought home the beer herself, making him aware who the gift came from.

***

I didn't admit to Jack that I was a daydreamer, building whole lives and schemes and relationships hourly in my head. Still, he understood it. In this we were alike. From time to time, while he was writing, he'd call to me with some problem.

"Look, I'm trying to convey here a feeling of... but I'm afraid it will be misunderstood as. . ." He'd read aloud. "You see what I mean? Is it clear to you?"

"Let me think about it and get back to you later," I'd say, and I'd go off by myself to imagine the same situation. I'd find my own description of it, write it down, cross it out, try it over and over, change the structure of the sentence, juxtapose, until there was nothing more to change. Then I'd take it to Jack.

"How does this sound?" I'd ask. And I'd read it to him.

More often than not, he'd say "That's not it!" or "I should know better than to ask a woman." And sometimes he'd use the idea in some way, and sometimes he wouldn't. Sometimes he'd argue about it and during the argument, he'd suddenly put into words what he'd been trying to say all along. I knew that it was our differences that made this possible. The introduction of a new perspective had value for him, even if it only served to make him object violently and clarify his stand.

"Aagh, women! Sentimental garbage! This is why women aren't writers!"

The insults didn't bother me, as long as I felt he'd listened.

* * *

The shoes I had bought too hastily the night of our wedding were giving me blisters, and every night after job hunting I traded them for bedroom slippers. Gabe demanded to see all my shoes, convinced there must be something else I could wear. But when she had looked through my collection of hiking boots, sandals, tennis shoes and spike-heeled pumps, she had to agree there was not a suitable pair among them.

On the way home from checking out a dental assistant job, which wouldn't begin until January, I visited the personnel office at May's Department Store to ask if they needed help during the Christmas rush. They did. What's more, they had an opening in the yard goods department and I could start tomorrow. I must have a black dress and black shoes, and I could purchase them at discount to be deducted from my first paycheck.

That night, I greeted Gabe with the news that I had a job, but before I had a chance to tell her the shoe problem was solved, she thrust a package into my hands and insisted I open it right away. Jack followed us into the kitchen, giving the package a knowing look. Gabe put her finger to her lips, hushing him. It was certainly a shoe box, and as I took off the lid, I saw what had to be the ugliest shoes ever made. They were fake red suede with a thick crepe sole extending for one inch all around the shoes, and they had more straps and buckles than any stretch of the imagination could possibly invent a use for.

"Put them on," Jack urged, trying to keep a straight face, and as I did so, an uncontrollable "ha—ha—ha!" escaped from him. He put his hands over his mouth, coughed and cleared his throat, but could do nothing about the shaking of his shoulders. Mirth finally exploded from him, and Gabe sent him from the room unceremoniously.

"Get out, you!"

I tried to express my gratitude while Jack's laughter, now verging on hysteria, reverberated through the apartment.

"You shouldn't have, Gabe," I resorted to, hoping she wouldn't know how literally I meant it. Her concern really did touch me. That she cared enough about my comfort to go to this trouble was surprisingly sweet.

"Ees no so much. No so very pretty, but ze best I find at ze factory. Ees just I want ze feet no hurt."

Bless her heart. In a rare demonstration of affection, I put my arms around her. We had such difficulty communicating with words.

"Gabe, you are so good to me," I said. "I love them and they are very comfortable. Thank you." I thought I understood in that moment what Jack had been trying to tell me about his mother. There was no doubt she did the best she could for those she loved.

If it sometimes came out harsh, sometimes tacky, and often short-sighted, that was never her intent.

Jack returned, having gained control of his laughter, but he lost it again momentarily when he saw the two of us embracing. Gabe grabbed a dishtowel and swatted him with it.

"You shut up, *fou!*"

"I'll wear them tomorrow, Gabe. Thank you very much." I put them back in the box and took them to the bedroom. Jack was sitting on the bed.

"You know why I was laughing, don't you?"

"I think so. Is it because you had to wear shoes like that all your life? Is that how you got the shoes you describe in your book?"

"That's part of it. But I can't tell you the good it does my soul to see you with your highfalutin ideas about what's fashionable having to wear those ugly canal boats and pretend you like them."

And I did wear them, down the stairs and out to the bus stop the next day, but I had stuffed my other shoes into my bag and I changed on the bus.

I kept track of my commissions in the yard goods department, and allowed myself to purchase the makings for Christmas presents out of these earnings. I fell in love with some blue cashmere the shade of Gabe's eyes and vowed she'd wear a blouse of it when she left to visit Caroline for the holidays. As my commissions added up, a blue tweed was purchased to go with the blouse, and a wool plaid in the muted tones Jack liked would make him a shirt. I declared the sewing room off limits, and spent every spare minute in there. Close to Christmas the store stayed open late, and I seldom got home before ten. One night, I found Jack more eager than usual to see me.

"I'm so glad you're home!" he said. "I've been wanting a spice cake so badly I could almost smell it baking in the oven. Would you make me one? With coffee icing?"

The late hours were catching up with me, and standing in the kitchen was the last thing I wanted to do.

"Do you know what *I've* been wanting?"

"What?" he asked, irritated that I would bother him with such trivia.

"A long soak in a hot tub and a good night's sleep."

"But you will make me the spice cake, won't you? I've been telling myself how lucky I am to have a sweet little wife who's a good cook, and I've been feeling sorry for all those poor devils out there who don't have a warm house with a kitchen and a good little wife to cook them things."

"Where's your mom?" If she had been home, the cake would be a reality.

"Union meeting," he explained tersely.

"Can't you make a cake?" I asked, heading for the bedroom.

"What? *Me* make a *cake*?"

I was beginning to feel that if I served any purpose at all in this household, it was to counteract Gabe's spoiling of her son.

"Well, I sure don't feel like it," I said. "And I don't think you should expect everybody to make sacrifices for your comfort all the time."

"A woman's comfort is dependent upon her husband's comfort," he informed me, dogmatically.

"Where did you get that idea?" I got my bathrobe from the closet and began to take off my clothes.

"And don't undress in front of me when you have no intention of doing anything about it."

"I didn't ask you to follow me in here," I said, putting on my bathrobe. "And I'm going to do something about it. I'm going to take a bath." I went into the bathroom and started the tub, pretending not to hear Jack as he stood outside the door complaining.

"You want a grumpy husband? That's what you'll have if you deny me some little thing like a spice cake. It wouldn't take you long to mix one up. Is it worth it to you to make me angry?"

Now I was determined not to give in. I went to bed in a huff and Jack made his irritation evident by slamming drawers, crumpling papers, and cursing the typewriter. I got up to close the door against the noise and Jack opened it instantly.

"Don't you close that door on me! That's my room too—and don't you forget it. And you're my wife! You'd better not forget that either!"

When Gabe's heavy, tired steps came up the stairs, I was still awake. I heard Jack's pleading and complaints in French and Gabe's consoling tones interspersed with references to *"La Belle,"* the name they both used for me when they were displeased. Before long the unmistakable aroma of spice cake floated from the kitchen.

* * *

Sunday night Gabe sent Jack to the store so she could speak to me privately while we fixed supper.

"Ti-Jeanne," she began, "ze woman always tired."

"Only if she's married," I countered.

"But when you love, ees a good tired. I love Jackie father. I love Jackie. You no love him yet."

We were having hot dogs for supper. I picked up a knife and sliced one in half lengthwise, intending to grill the halves.

Gabe took the knife from my hand, saying, "No. Like zees." She slashed another with three diagonal cuts halfway through. I shrugged and did the rest her way, without comment, wondering what motherly wisdom made her know that I didn't love her son.

"Eet's all right." She put her substantial arm around me. "You learn." I didn't know whether she referred to her kitchen procedures or loving Jack.

At supper I said little but watched Gabe and Jack more closely, more confused than ever about what constituted love. Gabe's love for Jack seemed to be a martyrdom designed to perpetuate his need for her and render him powerless without her. Is this what I would want for my children? I hoped I would put their needs above their wants, even if they turned against me as a result, but how did I know what I'd do in reality? Theory was so much closer to perfection than practice could ever be. Did love destroy objectivity? Did objectivity destroy love? Perhaps the two were just incompatible.

* * *

The weekend before Gabe left for North Carolina, I gave her a home permanent and we exchanged Christmas gifts. She put on her new clothes and admired herself in the full-length mirror.

"You look like a fine lady, Ma," Jack commented.

"She *is* a fine lady," I said.

"See? You *fou!*" Gabe cried triumphantly.

Since Jack would be lord of the manor for the holidays, he had been inviting everyone he knew, if not for dinner then for drinks, and if not for one day then for the next. I wanted to make pies. Gabe, who knew nothing of Jack's planned parties, worked long and patiently trying to teach me to make a good crust. I stood beside her and duplicated everything she did, measure for measure and movement for movement, and still, mine were failures and hers were excellent.

We saw Gabe off at Penn Station in a terrifying holiday crush. Borne along by the crowd, we struggled to stay together in the stream that surged toward her departure gate. Some had passed

out and were lifted above the mass to prevent their being tram-
pled. I had a terror of crowds. Gabe seemed so defenseless, I had
misgivings about her making the trip alone, but Jack assured me
she'd done it countless times and would be alright.

Just before she boarded the train she told me to look in the
freezer when I got home. When we got back, I immediately went
to look, and there were three perfect pie crusts just waiting to be
filled and baked.

"Oh Jack!" I called him into the kitchen. "Look what your
mom did!"

"I told you she loves you," he said.

The entire week was a party, culminating in a huge New Year's
Day dinner served to a crowd that lingered into the pre-dawn
hours. I disappeared to the kitchen at intervals, in an attempt to
keep up with the dishes. Only pots and pans remained when the
last guests had left.

"Come on to bed," Jack called. "Leave those till morning."

"I don't want to wake up to this mess," I said.

"Come on. You're on vacation. Stick them in the oven so you
won't have to see them." So that's what I did, and after giving the
table a quick wipe I got into bed to find him ready for me. Within
minutes he was finished and asleep, leaving me to wonder if I
should get up and do the pots and pans. While I wondered, I fell
asleep.

Gabe returned while we slept, two days ahead of schedule.
Before I was awake she had discovered the unwashed pots and
pans and was screaming for Jackie. He reached for his bathrobe,
cursing, and joined her in the kitchen. It was all in French but I
could almost understand it by now. *La Belle* this and *La Belle* that.
Was Jack excusing me, explaining, taking the blame? Vain hope!
He was commiserating. She had everything scrubbed and gleam-
ing by the time I entered the kitchen to face the music.

"Feelthy! Feelthy!" she raged, continuing to scrub the already shining counters. "We get *bugs*!"

"I'm sorry, Gabe," I said lamely, remembering the pie crusts she had left me. But she sighed and shook her head as though the damage were irreversible. I glared at Jack and went to get dressed, then left the house without breakfast and without telling anyone where I was going. Who cared? What did they need me for anyway? I felt depressed, exhausted, entirely unwanted. I resolved right that moment that I'd get a job in town, and yes, I'd move out. I couldn't bear this oppressive house and life any more.

The May's Christmas rush job was done, and it was a bad day for job hunting. The city was in slow motion, recuperating from New Year celebrations. I found an invitation to Sarah's showing in the mailbox when I got back to Gabe's, and I read it on the way upstairs. Jack met me at the door. "Where have you been?" he demanded.

"Job hunting." I kicked off my shoes as I sat down at the kitchen table.

"I wanted to go into town too," he said. "And I didn't have any money. Why didn't you tell me you were going?"

"Listen, Jack. My friend Sarah is having a fashion show on Saturday. Showing her own designs! I'd love to go, but how can I? Don't you think I want to go?"

"Why can't you go? You have subway fare, haven't you?"

"But it's not just a matter of subway fare. It's drinks, and maybe dinner afterward. I'm not in a position to carry my own weight. Don't you see?"

"Well, if she's a friend of yours, won't she buy your drinks?"

I started to answer him but changed my mind. He'd never understand why I couldn't go under those circumstances. I tried another tack.

"Let me ask you something. How are we ever going to get to

San Francisco if the money goes out as fast as it comes in?"

"It's too cold to go across the country now anyway. We'll make more money. I'll get a job too. You'll see."

No, you'll see, Jack! I shouted inwardly. *You're going to San Francisco alone!*

Job hunting continued without success. The longer I stayed in town, the more I spent on bus fare and coffee. I came home early one dismal January afternoon, cold and discouraged. Jack was out. I heated the coffee and sat at the table going over the ads once more.

Big deal! I'm going to make a life of my own, am I? Then what am I doing here? I'm more of a child here than I was in my own mother's house.

I missed Bill so much. And I wondered if I would ever meet anybody again who would know, so completely, what it means to be alive.

Chapter Seventeen

I heard footsteps on the stairs and got up, planning to take my coffee to the sewing room so I wouldn't have to talk to Jack. But instead, there was a knock on the door. I opened it warily.

There, hopping from one foot to the other, beaming his delight at having reached his destination at last, stood Neal Cassady. I recognized him instantly from the descriptions Jack had written of him.

"Neal! Come in!" I said.

"Ah, me, ah, me! So this is the little wife!" He came inside, dropped his gear and rubbed his gloveless hands in abandoned glee. "And where is *he*? The now honorable married man?"

I started to tell him Jack was out, but he said "No, don't wake him, little darling. Just show me where he is and I'll sit on his bed till he wakes. I've got nothing else to do now that I'm here. Oh, my feet! So sore!"

"He's not here, Neal. Come sit down. I just got home myself so I don't know where he is."

"Well, well! Not *here* you say. We'll just have to sit down then. That is definitely the first order of business. To sit down and take off the shoes. Oh, my poor, poor feet."

"Here, Neal. Let me take your coat. I'll hang it in the hall closet. And you could probably use something to eat."

"No, no." He handed me his coat. "When your good husband gets home will be soon enough."

"Some coffee? It's hot."

"Would there be, perchance, a cold beer? And as I was saying about my poor feet, what I could really use and would fully appreciate, my sweet darling, is a pair of your husband's clean socks, washed by your own lovely, slim young hands, no doubt. And because I couldn't put such precious socks on these dirty, sweaty, travel-sore feet, might I have a pan of warm water, some soap and a towel? The order of the aforementioned items doesn't matter, except for the beer. Let's start with that, shall we?"

It was impossible not to smile, to delight in the way Neal spoke. He might have sounded pompous, with his archaic expressions and run-on phrasing, but it all seemed so obviously tongue-in-cheek. He exaggerated a set of giddy mannerisms to an unforgettable extreme. I brought the requested articles and sat in fascinated silence as he immersed his feet and gulped his beer in rapturous comfort.

"Ah, ah. So good! How very warm this soak is. And how very good it is to be here. Let me tell you my dear, this last little bit of the trip just about finished me. Only thing that kept me going was my desire, my intense desire to see dear Jack and his sweet wife. And now here you are and here we are and you must, you absolutely must tell me all about your sweet young girlhood and how you came to love this great man who is now your husband."

I blinked. As he talked, the sound of Jack's proposal to me echoed in my memory. I had been unable until now to reconcile the audacity and presumptuousness he'd shown that night with the timid, suspicious personality I had now come to know so well. Now I saw that, in order to get the job done, and reinforced by the smoking of a lot of grass, Jack had become the embodiment of Neal. He had done it in the same way he automatically became W.C. Fields when he drank. The garb or disguise of one hero or another allayed his fears and suspicions and enabled him to surge forth and meet the challenge, whatever it was.

"Ah, it's so warm in here, and so cold, so damnably cold outside in this town. But never mind! We'll all soon be in San Francisco together. You, Carolyn, old Jack, and me. What times we'll have!"

He talked non-stop and there was so much energy about him he seemed to be jumping out of his skin.

"So you came to this big, confused city and found the man of your dreams. From some clean wind-swept state? Ah, yes. Oh, yes. I see it in your eyes, eyes that have looked at far horizons. Was it perchance Minnesota, land of sky blue waters, land of milk and honey?"

There was no need to answer him. He answered all his own questions with bigger-than-life, better-than-life answers. Now he drew his feet out of the water, and wrapped them in the towel, telling me of Texas, and how the nights felt and the stars looked and the air smelled. He was revving himself up in anticipation of Jack's arrival, talking of cars and escapades, jail memories and women and nights and blues.

And I wanted him to write it all down, or better yet record it. No matter how faithful the reproduction, I was sure text could never capture the vitality and intensity of the voice I now heard, describing everything in such a way that I lived it just by listening. He had the quality of a jazz musician inspiring the audience to answer with "yeah!" or to shout "go!" That quality in Neal's monologue was as elusive to the printed page as James Moody's horn. Sounds, sights and personalities came to life as he talked, assuming monumental proportions. Listening, I became aware of his phenomenal ability to perceive an event on several different levels and in terms of several disciplines at once, without losing the thread of one while he picked up another. To listen was to hear social commentary, poetry, philosophy, geography, and natural history.

We exchanged childhood stories. Watching him talk and expound and move, I remembered a sociology student I'd known, who had told me officiously that all who resist the socialization process will wind up either in prison or in a mental institution. He believed that no individual was capable of forming a behavior code or a value system without society's dictum. His arrogant pronouncement had infuriated me, yet I realized how close I had come to mental illness in creating the superficial character I inhabited, trying to escape detection as a social anarchist.

And here was Neal, raw and alive. Not the well-mannered, numbed excuse for a living being that I was. Had he experienced ostracism and revised his outward behavior? I doubted it, but then he'd spent time in jail.

"Did you find it hard to resist the mold?" I asked him.

"I'm sure it was harder for you, my dear," he said. "I had nothing to resist. No mold was presented to me until it was too late. The die was cast."

"I'm glad," I said. "And I'm glad Jack has a friend like you. But if the world were inhabited by people like you and me, there'd be no order at all. Do you ever think about that?"

"Ah, but it isn't, you see." He laughed. "And this is by a divine design. We have our place."

"I haven't found mine."

"Well, neither have I. But it doesn't matter. The place is there whether we recognize it or not."

I smiled. "But don't you think we might be more useful if we recognized it?"

"Ah, now there's the question. There's the question. You and Carolyn would find a lot to talk about. You have the same philosophic bent. To me it doesn't matter. I just do it."

At the sound of footsteps on the stairs I took away the pan, towel and soap. "I'll put your socks in with Jack's laundry," I told Neal.

He put his finger to his lips and took his shoes to the bedroom.

I opened the door as Jack arrived. Peering at my face, he asked "What are you looking so mysterious about?"

I didn't answer but stepped back to let him in, wanting to see his face when he saw Neal. He put out his hand to touch a familiar object, a book of Neal's left on the desk. His eyes widened as Neal came padding out of the bedroom in sock feet. The complete abandon with which Jack dropped the things he had been carrying, and his shouted "*Nee*—hul" with a catch in his throat like a sob, told me that *this*, if anyone, was the being Jack loved more than himself.

They slapped each other on the back and laughed and shouted till they almost cried. "You old devil!" "You bastard, you!" "Son of a gun!"

I went to the kitchen to start dinner, leaving them in a confusion of punches and hugs like two puppies on the couch.

"How about some beer in here!" Jack called, and it was delivered.

"How long can you stay, Neal?" he asked.

"I planned on a week."

"All right! I am entirely at your disposal, except for one night when we're going to the Duke Ellington concert with Henri Cru. Remember the crazy Marseillaise I told you about?"

"Well, ahem. Yes, of course, but I want to spend some time with Allen too. You understand that, dear Jack. Tonight though, *tonight!* I just want to dig you and your wife in your marriage situation and we'll get our plans together for your trip, because I will hear no excuses. You'll have to live not just near us but absolutely next door, or failing that, in the same house. So happy for you, man! And she's thin! Remember what I told you about skinny girls? They're the best! And wasn't it a delight to get to know her body? All of it, starting from the toes, I mean. Do you see what I meant now? There's nothing like knowing, I mean really *knowing* a woman."

"Yeah, yeah," Jack said uncertainly. "Hey man, don't you want to go into town tonight? Look up some people, find some girls? After dinner, of course."

It would have been impossible not to hear the conversation. I came to the doorway to get Jack's attention.

"Your mother's late. I wonder what's keeping her."

"Union meeting again. There's trouble at the factory."

"Isn't that luck?" Neal asked me. "Gabe thinks I'm leading her only son astray. And she's right, of course. Quite right. Quite right. Ahem! If she were here she'd hasten my departure, would-n't she, Jack?"

I assumed there would be three for dinner and got back to the stove. Their conversation continued in hushed tones until they came to stand in the doorway, Neal a little behind Jack, nudging him, whispering "Go on!" and pushing him toward me in the manner of one little boy urging another to ask his mom if they can have some cookies.

"Neal, you're staying for dinner, aren't you?" I asked.

"Oh, yes! Dinner!" he said, pushing Jack a little farther.

Jack finally came up to me and said, "Ah... I want to talk to you. Come into the bedroom for a minute." I checked the stove to be sure I wouldn't burn anything, and followed him into the bed-room, passing Neal, who rocked on his heels, beaming at our departure.

Jack sat on the edge of the bed and motioned to me to sit beside him.

"Now, darling," he began. I immediately gave him a highly suspicious look, because he had never called me that before.

"What I want to ask is this...You find Neal attractive, don't you?"

"He's very unusual and interesting. I enjoy listening to him."

"Never mind that!" he said. "He's physically attractive to you, isn't he?"

"Not particularly."

"Ah, g'wan. He is too. Anyway, he finds *you* very attractive."

"I'm flattered." I was beginning to get the picture. "Let's go have dinner." I stood up to go.

"Now wait a minute. Listen, please. Neal's like a brother to me. We've always shared everything and... , well, I want you to know that if you and Neal... , well, you'd have my permission. That is, it wouldn't bother me a bit if... , well, I'd be proud." He lost confidence and stammered at the rage he saw growing in me.

"*You're* giving *me* permission to sleep with Neal?"

"Shh!"

"I don't need your permission. It isn't yours to give. If I wanted someone else I'd just leave you. It would be that simple."

"Now wait. I don't mean like that. I'd be with you, of course. The three of us together. Please. He wants to and we've done this before. It's nothing new for Neal and me. You see, there's no jealousy between us. You have to understand what a great buddy, what a great brother he is to me. Be reasonable. Don't insult him, please."

I tried to soften a bit. I could see what he was going through. He was under the strongest kind of peer pressure. He had followed Neal in every scheme, every prank, every wild drive and chase after women, and he was afraid he'd be diminished in Neal's eyes if he stopped here. Neal's curiosity about his friend's wife was understandable. Probably more men experienced that curiosity than ever voiced it or satisfied it. But it was not my problem. I certainly didn't feel the kind of slavish loyalty to Jack that might have made a *menage a trois* possible, though Jack would have loved to be able to say, "Look. My woman will do anything I want her to."

"I understand, Jack, and I won't feel any jealousy if you and Neal take a subway into town and find a girl you can share. You're free." And I couldn't help adding a little nastily, "I give you my permission."

"But it wouldn't be the same. It's because you're my wife that he wants you."

"I understand that too. But Jack, last November when you realized that I was the 'Cathy' Bill had been talking about, you must have known that nothing like what you have in mind could ever take place."

"I would have thought that a girl like Bill described would have been amenable to her husband's wishes by now! Listen, Neal is a great lover. Women just fall in love with him after one night. He could show you what it's all about... probably show me what I'm doing wrong. Just be agreeable. Everything will be much better for us as a result. You'll see. It'll be alright."

"Jack, the last thing I want is to know what it's all about."

"Oh, why do you have to be such a goddamned prude!"

"Because not all A are B," I said coldly. "Shall we have dinner? You can show your friend what a great domestic your wife is, and he'll never have to know she's a lousy lay."

"To hell with dinner!" he said, going back to the living room and slamming the door. "Damned haughty broad!" he shouted to Neal. "If I were any kind of a man I'd beat her."

"Now, now. That's no way to talk," Neal reasoned with Jack. "Why, you should be proud that she's so loyal. I'm disappointed, of course. Would have liked to know the delights you find in such a sweet girl. But I'm so happy for you, dear Jack. No matter! We'll go to the big city and we'll have a ball. But why forsake dinner? Make up to her, old man, and tell her you love her. You'll have to do it sooner or later."

I decided to make an appearance rather than sulk. Jack was sulky enough for both of us, and Neal was being the man of the two.

"No offense intended, Neal," I said. "Let's not let the food get cold."

"I don't hold it against you in the least, my girl. Ahem, no pun intended. Your prerogative I'm sure, and my loss, though I have been told by certain ladies that, ah, well, it was worth the trip. Your devotion to your husband is completely understood. Yes! Even admired, I might say. Now Jack, let's enjoy this lovely meal your wife has prepared."

Jack was sullen through dinner, not looking at me, as Neal told endless stories of his travels and played his flute. I was more relaxed than I had been in a long, long time. If Jack could give me permission to sleep with Neal, he could hardly object if I made my liking for him obvious by speaking to him and laughing with him. And could Neal misinterpret my animation? Now that we knew where we stood, communication was direct and comfortable.

Neal was working on the Southern Pacific Railroad and had come all the way across the country on his pass, a change from hopping freights and hitching rides. There was no doubt in my mind that the man was brilliant, with no use for a formal education. He was all the more alive and raw for not having had a benefit like that. By avoiding education, Neal Cassady had managed to retain that inborn knowledge of how to survive and love every minute of it.

We sat after dinner and lingered over coffee for hours, and Jack eventually lost his dark mood as the life at the table won out. As soon as he began to participate, I sat back and watched. He had become more interesting to me since Neal's arrival. I was witnessing the difference between *The Town And The City* and *On The Road*, the difference between the brooding Ti-Jean and the laughing, charming Jack I had seen at Lucien's party, the difference between the shy man who wanted an unworldly wife and the adventurous man who wanted a sexually liberated party girl.

I wondered about the forces that had brought these two together, and about the exchanges between them. An obvious product of their meeting was Jack's book in progress. But what effect had Jack had upon Neal? There was no way for me to know, since my knowledge of him was after the fact.

I wondered what kind of a writer Jack would have become had he not met Neal. I had seen some of Neal's letters to Jack—no, Jack had read portions of them to me. I knew that pieces of those letters had to remain private. I secretly believed that only Neal could write like Neal. But would his writings portray his essential quality, or did Jack find it necessary to immortalize him with his own stylistic patina?

They were talking now about boxcars they had known and shared. And Neal spoke of boxcars he had shared with his father and other hoboes long before that. As I listened I could hear the train whistle and the sound of the cars coupling in the yard, and I could smell the cars, see the wheat fields in the dawn and dew passing by, just as though I were watching from the open door of a boxcar. I could see Omaha, and hear the conductor in the passenger cars calling it out as a stop, *"Oh...maha. Oma—hah? Ohhh...ma—ha."*

And not for the first time, I regretted not having been born a male. This was the closest I could come to it, sitting in the company of men, with a relationship (or lack of one) established, so there was no need or place for the usual male-female games. Just real talk about real things and real experiences.

Soon, though, they tired of talk, remembering that other need that must be satisfied, the one I would have no part in, because I couldn't be a companion. Only a tool.

* * *

Jack and I waited at Henri Cru's apartment for the limousine that would take us to the Duke Ellington concert at Carnegie Hall. I had thought the limousine was being rented in the nature of a joke, and I had hoped that Henri's tie, hand-painted with replicas of our tickets, was a joke, too. But here was Henri, wearing the tie in front of his mirror, rolling the edge of his pink shirt collar between his fingers to get it to lie just right, exquisitely. And neither Jack nor Henri saw that it was obscene.

"Don't you see this as an insult to the Duke?" I asked Jack.

"Look. Dig Henri," he said, smiling at the reflection, not even hearing me. "See how he has to get that collar to roll just so? Nothing haphazard for old Henri! He's a perfectionist."

"Some day the importance of little details will be meaningful to you, Jack, dear boy," Henri said. "You'll put your dreadful plaid shirts aside in favor of silk ones."

"But I'm not wearing a plaid shirt tonight, Henri. Don't you think this is appropriate?" He pulled at the front of his white dress shirt.

"It's acceptable, but not unique. One day the ordinary will not be good enough for you."

"You sound like my wife, for crying out loud," Jack said.

"I resent that," I objected. "There's a difference between distinction and vulgarity." Henri looked at me suspiciously in the mirror, and Jack wanted it spelled out.

"You're distinctive and he's vulgar?"

"Let's just say that Henri aspires to the subtle insult." I was relieved when Henri smiled in agreement. "Not that he succeeds," I added.

His date sat on the edge of her chair, uncomfortably stuffed into something grotesquely fashionable. Even if it had been tastefully done, what was to be gained by this superficial display? How far could a phony image go in terms of self-respect?

Three short rings told Henri the limousine was ready, and we went downstairs to be helped into it by the chauffeur. As we pulled away from the curb, Neal came running across the street to hang on Jack's door. The chauffeur had to stop to avoid dragging him into traffic, though the look on his face said he would have liked to do just that. Jack opened the window and hastily introduced Neal to Henri, who pointedly ignored him.

"Hey, Jack! Can't you give me a lift to 42nd Street?" Neal rubbed his hands together, his breath visible in the frosty night. "I'm about to freeze my balls off in this durned cold." Jack looked at Henri for an answer, but all he got was a quick negative shake of the head and a look of displeasure.

"No, man. I'm sorry. Can't do it," Jack said, and Neal turned without a word and ran up the street in the direction we were heading, his thin coat flapping behind him in the wind.

"That's a lousy way to say goodbye to a friend," I said.

"But it's not *time* for saying goodbye to Neal, don't you see?" Jack answered impatiently. "I've already done that. It's time for the concert now. And there's no way to put the two things together."

I had a fleeting vision of the four of us in our absurd finery, bearing Neal into Carnegie Hall on our shoulders, like a hero in rags. That was the only way I could see all this pomp serving any purpose.

"Couldn't Neal come to the concert with us?" I asked Henri.

"No, no!" he said emphatically. "Absolutely out of the question."

How sad, how unspeakably sad that anyone should need these props to enjoy a night of good music. Neal would have enjoyed it in his ragged old coat, and I was sure that if the Duke had compared Neal's appreciation with Henri's, he would have chosen the threadbare wild man. Too much of life was like this, expensive wrappings attempting to compensate for the poverty of contents.

Too bad, Neal, old buddy. It's not time for someone real like you. You'd spoil our make-believe, reminding us that we're all cold, much of the time, in a thin coat on a winter street.

Chapter Eighteen

With that searingly memorable image, of Neal hurling himself down a Manhattan street alone, Jack would close the long story he told in *On The Road*. And the more I thought about my life with Jack Kerouac, the more the episode took on an air of finality for me as well. I dreamed, once, that I was the one who had run from the limousine in the night.

I wanted this unhappy interval in both our lives to come to an end. Jack and I hung on, day to day, not clinging, just whirled together and unable to see the way out. I didn't wonder anymore if I would stay with him forever. I only wondered how, and when, the whole thing would fall apart.

It never even occurred to me that Jack might be more determined than I was to keep our marriage together.

***

I poured pudding into bowls and set them on the counter to cool. It was Friday night, and almost time for Gabe to get home, but Jack wanted to go into the city.

"How much money do we have left?" he asked.

187

"Very little," I told him, unsympathetic and unwilling to give him the actual information. "We can't spend any more till I get a job. I don't know how much I'm going to have to use for carfare."

"You don't have to work in the city. If you get a job in the neighborhood you won't have to worry about carfare. How much is there?"

"Never mind." I scraped the pudding bowl with a spatula, determined not to get caught up in this game.

"Don't you never mind me!" Jack shouted. "Aren't you living here rent-free? Aren't you eating my mother's food? Don't I share what I have with you?"

"Sure, as long as it's your mother's," I answered icily.

"What's my mother's is mine. Think about that when you sit down to dinner tonight!" As he yelled to the opposite wall, I peered at him. I knew what he would do next, knew with utter certainty, and Jack didn't disappoint me. He turned abruptly on his heel to stride out of the room, looking back at me over his shoulder, eyebrows coming together in an accusing frown, lower lip thrust out in a pout, the large vein at his temple pulsating visibly. I had the unsettling sense that I was seeing his movements before he made them, so familiar was this gesture to me. He jerked his head sideways, muttering that deep-throated growl, "Aagh." And he shook his right lower arm downward, palm toward me, as if he was shaking water off his hand.

I stared him out of the room, filled with secret delight and determination. I had paid particular attention to his little show this time. Now I was determined never to see it again.

I changed to my bathrobe and pajamas, and when Gabe came in, I met her in the kitchen to tell her I had an upset stomach and wouldn't want any dinner. She followed me into the bedroom to take my temperature. I was never sick, and Gabe knew it. She gazed at me fretfully, trying to puzzle it out.

"It's just my stomach," I said. "No fever. I just have to sleep."

Jack knew very well what was going on, but if he let on to Gabe, I was unaware of it. I intended to stay in bed until Monday morning and never eat a bite of food in this house again. I wanted Jack to witness my abstinence.

But he managed to talk his mother into giving him the money to get to town, and he didn't return home that night. On Saturday morning, Gabe came in to interrogate me.

"You have fight weez Jackie?"

I nodded. She had to know sooner or later, and in Jack's absence, I gave in and let it be sooner.

"You tell me," she demanded. "If Jackie hurt you I never forgive."

"No," I said. I looked at Gabe tiredly, and suddenly felt I could not put my unhappiness into the simple English words she would understand. "It's just a little thing, not important."

"He say somesing bad to you? What?"

I shook my head, unable to express it at all, even with gestures. All I wanted, all I was determined to do, was to get out, and one way was as good as another. But Jack and Gabe—they would still have to live with each other, after all. It wouldn't matter what had happened between Jack and me. No matter what I said, no matter how bad I felt, Jack could make himself look good in Gabe's eyes. She had produced and nurtured him, he protected and took care of her, and in the end she would believe that he was the genius whose wishes must be fulfilled.

Gabe went back to the kitchen, leaving me faced with the bare irony and ultimate stupidity of my little game. Jack was depriving me of my intended audience. Yet he would come home eventually and I was stubbornly determined that he wasn't going to find me at the table breaking my fast. I clung to my plan inflexibly, feeling a little guilty for making Gabe miserable, and knowing that it didn't make a bit of difference to Jack whether I ate or not.

He didn't come home Saturday night either, and Gabe was worried sick. Now she accused me of driving her son away.

"Don't worry about him," I said wearily. "He's at Lucien's, if he's not up to something worse."

I had time to myself, had the whole bed to myself, and could have enjoyed the weekend if I hadn't been so hungry. Unless I counted my Friday morning coffee, the fast had begun Thursday night. I drank water but it didn't ease the tension. The least household noise made me jump as if my nerves had been sprung.

I stayed awake, woozy and filled with agonizing looping self-awareness, long after Gabe went to bed. Finally, late into the night, I began to feel calm. My head was light and I was engulfed in a deep, surreal sense of timelessness. I remembered that feeling from my childhood. It was a prelude to hallucinations, and I began to look around for the Japanese fish kite.

* * *

Sunday afternoon when Jack showed up, Gabe demanded to know why he had not come home to his sick wife.

"*Elle n'est pas malade* (she's not sick)", he said.

"*Si elle ne mange pas, elle va mourir!* (If she doesn't eat, she'll die.)"

He came into the bedroom and said to me, "Will you knock it off? You've got my mom all upset. She thinks you're going to die."

"I *want* to die!" I wailed, and I almost meant it. I was so hungry I could faint. Gabe was making chicken soup and the smell was driving me crazy. She came in with a bowl of the wonderful stuff.

"Hold ze hands," she instructed Jack, and as he did so, she pried open my not-very-resistant mouth and spooned the soup in.

"First you eat," she said. "*Zen* you die."

* * *

Finally, thankfully, I found a job Monday at Stouffer's, lunch and dinner shift—so I wouldn't have to eat at home. On my afternoon breaks I looked for an apartment, saving my tips so I'd have the deposit in hand when I found something. Within two weeks I had the rent paid on a studio apartment at 454 West 20th Street, and enough left over for the move. I went to a Village moving company and made arrangements, telling them to take everything in the sewing room. I even drew them a floor plan so they could find it without knocking on doors and waking people. The date was set and at the appointed hour, during my break, I hurried to the new address to see my things and collect my key. I hadn't said a word to Jack or to Gabe. I wanted out, out without complications. I was willing to do whatever it took to have an independent life, to be a free and single woman, to be nobody's wife once again.

I saw the moving truck from two blocks away and ran toward it, but as I approached, what I saw on the sidewalk made me stop in my tracks.

There sat Jack on his desk in his sheepskin slippers, his morning face scowling at me under disheveled hair.

"What's going on here?" I asked him.

"That's what I was about to ask you."

"Well, obviously I've moved out, but I hadn't intended to take you with me."

"He says he's your husband," said the driver. "I told him he'd have to wait outside till you confirmed his story."

"Then what?" I asked.

"Then I'll give him the key. Husbands have rights, you know."

"Do you mean I can't have my own apartment?"

"Look, lady, I'm not a lawyer. But unless you have a court order, you can't keep your husband out of your home. And vice versa."

"Come on. Let's get off the street before we draw a crowd," Jack said.

"He's my husband," I admitted reluctantly.

"Okay," the driver said. "That'll be ten dollars more for the desk."

"Ten dollars!"

"Don't complain. I moved your husband for free."

"Thanks a lot." I shot daggers at Jack and handed over the additional ten. The desk was carried upstairs.

"I'm your husband. Remember?" Jack glanced at me briefly, then looked away, his arms folded. "You can't walk out on me."

I didn't know what to say. I wanted to blurt out to him, "What are you doing here? You can't be any happier with this marriage than I am." Instead I just stood on the sidewalk, glaring at him.

"You can give me that key now," he said to the driver when he came downstairs.

"Sorry, lady," the driver said, as he handed Jack the key. "Next time try moving to another state." He drove away, leaving our furniture and our fortunes behind.

I looked quizzically at Jack, but he didn't seem to have anything to say, for once. Finally I told him, "I have to get back to work. If you go out, please lock up."

"Don't worry about it," he said glumly. "My manuscript's in there. It's the most important thing in my life."

I started back uptown, walking slowly, trying to reconcile myself to the fact that I hadn't closed the book on this disastrous marriage after all. I lectured myself as I walked, and I began gaining confidence, assuring myself, *Things won't be the same any more.* As I walked on, I lifted my head to that determination. And nothing would be the same.

* * *

Seymour Wyse, a friend of Jack's since his days in school, was working at a store called the Esoteric Record Shop near the new apartment. He had the most charmingly crass English accent. Jack loved to waste pleasant hours in the back of the shop listening to great jazz cuts that Seymour would play for him, songs nobody had ever heard. One evening I met them both there after my shift. I was glancing over the paycheck I'd received that day from Stouffer's.

Jack held out his hand for it, not speaking over the music, his head nodding to the beat of the hi-hat.

I shook my head, similarly wordless, folding the check and putting it into my pocket. Seymour's eyes followed this little pantomime, registering Jack's irritated reaction.

"Let me have the paycheck," Jack directed me.

"No," I told him, full of resolve. "I earned it."

"You've got your tip money. Let me have the wages. I have groceries to buy. You haven't put a thing in the refrigerator."

I sat down, smoothing the skirt of my uniform. "You're going to be buying your own groceries now," I told him. "Or eat at your mother's, I don't care. I have my meals at work." Just to aggravate him, I patted my stomach. "I had a very filling meat loaf platter this evening."

"Damn!" Jack said to Seymour, who simply grinned at my audacity. Jack held out his hand again. "Give me that paycheck, *now!*"

"No."

"I'll open a joint checking account for us."

"No, you won't."

He shook his hand in frustration. "Just *give* it to me!"

"No!" I exploded. "Jack, I'm not going to do this! We could fight like pre-adolescent siblings when we were at your mother's house, but we're done with that now. Grow up! Act your age, pull

your weight." I rushed ahead before he could ridicule me for my cliches. "We're not going to have any joint accounts. I'm not going to put food onto your table or into your stomach or between your sheets! And I am sick of your selfish, childish behavior!"

Jack's face was a furious red, but he looked at Seymour and managed to calm down. I shut my mouth and long moments passed, punctuated by reeds and piano on the phonograph, while Jack returned to a more natural color. When he finally spoke, it wasn't to me, but to his friend, in tones of amazement.

"What am I doing wrong?" Jack asked Seymour. "Where does she get off, talking to *me*, her husband, like that?"

Seymour shrugged with a half-smile. It was the most obvious thing in the world to him. "You got to bring home the bycon, Jack. That's what it is. Bring home the bycon."

He looked at me, and Jack looked at me, and I nodded without adding a word.

* * *

Jack decided it was worth a try, so he got a job with 20th Century Fox, summarizing screenplays. He would read a script, write a summary, and then the Fox executives wouldn't have to bother reading it. For all I know, they had somebody else summarizing the summaries. But the job was made to order for Jack because he could work at home, when he wanted to, spending as much time as he wanted on his own writing.

With both of us working, he now insisted we make a financial arrangement: I would buy the groceries and he'd pay the rent. I reluctantly agreed, though I was sure in my heart that his job wouldn't last.

Seymour visited often, along with Jack's other friends, and even though they kept Jack from getting much work done, they were welcome guests. One afternoon, on my day off, Jack, Allen Ginsberg, and Seymour were at the apartment. We were all laughing and enjoying ourselves.

"Hey!" Jack cried excitedly. "I know what let's do. Let's go down to the waterfront and climb around on the docks!"

I loved the idea, and I ran excitedly to get a sweater to go out with them.

"Not *you*!" Jack said. "You'd only be in the way, and you'd probably get hurt."

I felt crushed. It had sounded like such fun. Nothing else would do now but to be on the water, so I went to Central Park and rented a rowboat, alone.

On Jack's first payday, we saw Helen Parker and Yale Harrison off to Mexico at a little bar near Penn Station. Jack called for round after round, until his cash was gone. Inevitably, he now asked for the grocery money. I tried to withhold it, but he was in no condition to listen to practical arguments.

"Just be glad we have it!" he said.

Walking home with Allen and John Holmes, we passed a sidewalk stand of spring's first asparagus.

"Ahh. Look at that!" Jack exclaimed. His voice was full of exhilaration. "Let's get some for dinner."

"Jack," I told him. "There's no money left."

"What?! I can't have spring's first asparagus?" He turned off Ninth Avenue abruptly, striding angrily away from us.

Holmes, Allen, and I looked at each other and shrugged. We continued back to the apartment by the usual route.

By the time we got there, Jack was waving us in with a quart of beer, finger in the air, W.C. Fields-style.

***

I was reading a letter from my mother the next morning before work, lingering over a cup of coffee at the kitchen table. Jack came into the room with his arms full. He'd brought me six pairs of socks, rolled into neat balls, and he now dumped them onto the table beside my coffee.

"I go into a new order of socks now," he said.

"Hmm?" I wasn't really paying attention.

"Spring," he elaborated.

"Spring." I finally looked up from my letter in mild exasperation. "Spring?"

"These are too heavy now," Jack said. "I want you to put them away somewhere."

"What's wrong with keeping them in your drawer? We haven't any place to store things here."

"No. I don't want them in my drawer. My mom always put the winter clothes away for the summer. You could put them in a box in the closet."

"So could you," I pointed out. He was turned away from me and pretended not to hear this bit of household logic, but an unsuppressed flick of the wrist—shaking me off—gave him away.

"And when you go out," he added, "get me maybe four more pairs of lightweight socks."

"What size?" I asked.

He was completely taken aback. "How should I know what size? The same size these are, for krissake."

I watched his back. I could not honestly believe that he didn't know his sock size, but I wanted to know more. "Jack? What size shirt do you wear?"

He turned to me, tugged at the wrist of his shirt, made a face without answering and turned his back again.

"What size shoes?"

"I don't know what size socks or shirts or shoes, damn it! I don't need to know. It is my wife's responsibility to take care of that information for me."

I smiled. "What size underwear?"

"Aagh!" he answered, twisting his head and flicking his hand visibly this time, as he went out the door.

His mother had always done his shopping, and now he left the house, leaving his wife responsible for gathering the information necessary to the storage and purchase of his socks.

I cleared the table, preparing to answer my mother's letter, and two of the sock rolls fell to the floor. I picked them up, considered them, then tucked them into the fruit bowl, laying the bananas over them.

I hadn't finished more than ten lines to my mother before Jack rushed back through the door. He looked upset, out of breath, and he held out his hand. He was holding his tie, but it had been dismembered. The knot was still tied around his neck.

"Steen cut off my tie!" he shouted.

I tried to find out what had happened, but Jack evaded my questions. The best explanation I could get was that Steen had "failed to show proper respect" for Jack's married state when inquiring about my health.

Apparently, they'd crossed paths just down the block; instead of saying, "Good morning, Jack! How are you? And how's your wife?," Steen had simply said "Hi Jack! How's Joan?" For Jack, this implied an unacceptable familiarity. An argument had followed.

Jack insisted no punches had been thrown. I could not manage to determine how the knot had managed to lose its tie, then. They had certainly been securely attached to each other when Jack left the house. But I let it go.

"He said he loves you more than I do!" Jack cried indignantly.

"Well, he probably does."

"What!?"

I looked at Jack so flustered and frightened, and regretted opening my mouth then. I knew I couldn't explain. How could I ever make him understand? I knew Jack didn't love me, I knew it in my bones. We were only together as a convenience, a habit, and one that couldn't last. Steen, at least, thought of me as a friend, a playmate. We had played on the docks together, where Jack thought I'd just get in the way. Who had ever loved me? Maybe Herb had. Maybe Bill Cannastra had. But maybe, I believed it was quite possible, nobody ever had.

"Oh, Jack, don't worry," I soothed. "He doesn't love me. No, he doesn't love me at all."

That was all it took to calm him.

* * *

Jack's brother-in-law, Paul Blake, came to New York. Gabe was moving to North Carolina. I didn't ask, but I had to wonder how Ti-Nin felt about that. I remembered her fiercely whispered words to Jack, the first time I'd met her: "Don't you dare go off and get married and leave Ma alone again. She'll come and stay with us!"

But there was no word from Ti-Nin. Jack was enlisted to assist in the move. He went south with his mother and her belongings, and stayed for a week.

The peace and solitude were a gift to me. I spent luxurious hours alone, indulging in my own thoughts. I tried to focus on the future. I had stopped, long ago, expecting the marriage to last—but what would be next for me? All my reasons for marrying in the first place had proven to be pipe dreams. Even my dream of having children now felt sour. I didn't want anything to happen that would serve to perpetuate this sad, purposeless union. I'd been fitted for a diaphragm, and we kept it in the sock drawer.

Marian Holmes came to visit one afternoon. I talked to her about how badly I wanted more out of life. "You know, I'd really like to go to college," I told her. "I've been thinking about enrolling at CCNY in the fall."

"Well, what a marvelous idea, Joan!" Marian encouraged. "What would you study?"

"I was thinking about... genetics," I answered, a little shyly. "I'm interested in it. It's something I'd like to know about, for my own information." I thought of my grandfather, and my friend Sarah, and realized how much I wanted to make them both proud.

Marian must have read some different, psychological meaning into my interest, because she answered by asking me, "How's your sex life with Jack?"

I looked at her and fumbled for a word. "Unremarkable," I finally told her, for lack of a better description.

"I'm not surprised," Marian smiled. "Jack's a minute man."

I just shook my head.

The mail arrived while Marian was sipping coffee. A letter from Jack was mixed in the stack, and I pulled it out apprehensively. I bit my lip as I stared at the postmark. "He's writing to say he's staying in North Carolina," I predicted as I opened it.

But instead, I read Jack's words: "I've been thinking of you and of our life together. It's sweet and I love you."

I showed Marian the letter, and she smiled and got up to leave without saying a word.

For the rest of the day I beat up on myself for my eagerness to leave, my lack of faith in Jack, my feeling that marriage was nothing more than a prison. I resolved to try harder with Jack, to go halfway, to try to help us both get something out of our life together.

He came home to New York that evening, and I made us an elegant pasta dinner, served with a tablecloth and wine. Afterward I told him my plan to improve myself by going to college classes in the fall. Jack seemed to listen until I got to a certain word.

"Genetics!" He laughed. "Genetics! You want to smart-ass around, that's all you want to do. Genetics! Ha! There's only one thing you could study that would do you any good. Home ec!" I stared at him, my jaw tight, remembering with a physical flood of anger why I wanted to get out.

The emotional reconciliation in my mind had lasted about four hours. I'd know better than to fool myself that way again.

Chapter Nineteen

On a sloppy wet evening in early April, I came home from work tired and worn, to find Jack staring unhappily and silently at his typewriter.

I had found a better waitressing job at the new Brass Rail on Park Avenue and 41st. All the help was new, including Puerto Rican bus boys just off the plane, some speaking no English at all. For two weeks prior to opening we were trained in heavy silver service, tray on the shoulder. I laughed aloud on the night of the grand opening when the first two letters on the neon sign failed to light up. From that night on, I would always remember that restaurant as the "Ass Rail."

Jack seemed to have been locked in some struggle with *On The Road* through my whole training period. He wasn't writing, and he wasn't talking much, either. He asked broad, grasping questions about style, about structure. They seemed thoroughly irrelevant to me. Neal was spontaneous. The words should simply come out. They should spill onto the page without control, finding style and structure in the telling.

I sat down across from Jack and looked tiredly back at him. "What was it like, Jack?" I finally asked, after a long silence.

"To be on the road with Neal?"

"Yes, what happened, what really happened?"

I started asking questions. Questions about Neal, about traveling, cities, trains, New York, Mexico, cars, roads, friends, Neal, Neal, Neal, and Neal.

"Jack," I asked him again, "what really happened? What did you and Neal really do?"

The questions, after a time, seemed to ignite some spark in Jack. He went back to his typewriter, and now he typed with accelerating speed, pounding keys, late into the night. When I got up in the morning, I saw that the clothes he had dropped on the floor were soaked with sweat. And I saw that there were feet and feet of the teletype roll, filled with dense typescript, hanging off the back of the typewriter now.

I was glad Jack was writing again. It improved his mood immeasurably. I knew it was ironic that I acted as his muse and his inspiration when his writing had always been so unimportant, even unreadable, to me. But it was such a relief to have him focused on something other than his own boredom and selfish needs.

For the next few weeks, I became accustomed again to sleeping while Jack typed. I only woke if it stopped suddenly. That happened one night, May 10, 1951, and the consequences would change both our lives forever.

Jack was in his bathrobe, behind the screen that surrounded his desk, typing furiously. The typing stopped. I opened my eyes, and almost immediately he emerged.

"Quick!" he said, dropping his bathrobe and pulling the covers off me. A brief argument ensued: spontaneity vs. preparedness. Spontaneity won, and the diaphragm stayed buried with the socks.

Two minutes later, Jack rolled over and went to sleep. I knew I wasn't responsible for his arousal, and I got up to see what was in the typewriter. I found my answer in his description of Terry, the Mexican girl he knew in California, and the pity he felt for her. Remembering other occasions when I hadn't been able to understand what precipitated his sudden inspiration, it all hung together. There was always an element of the pathetic, or the downtrodden, or abject poverty and misery, either in the conversation or in something or someone he'd seen. I had never allowed him to see anything of that sort in me. I would not acknowledge my own weakness or pain and I never cried. So I had nothing to do with his arousal. I was merely the receptacle. This was the time, though, that the receptacle turned out not to be empty.

* * *

In late June I began to think I was pregnant. Apprehensively, unhappily, I told Jack. He was sure I was mistaken, but he sent me to Ti-Nin's obstetrician, and the doctor confirmed my suspicion.

Jack was still unbelieving. He couldn't accept the idea. Not that he didn't want children. It just wasn't the right time. The book wasn't finished. He talked about Neal's irresponsibility, bringing all those kids into the world without making any provision for them.

"Nine months is enough time for two people to prepare for a baby," I answered him. "I can work till my seventh month, anyway."

"The preparation should have been before the fact. Where was your diaphragm?"

"It was that night you wouldn't let me get up," I let him know.

"That's no excuse. A woman should always be prepared."

"That would be ridiculous, Jack, considering how seldom there's a need."

He gave me one of his dark looks and asked, "How far along are you? Did the doctor say?"

"About seven weeks."

"That's early!" he said. "We can get something done. It would be cheaper in the long run."

I didn't respond, just looked intently at him.

"What's the matter with you?" He was exasperated.

"It's out of the question, Jack."

"Look, this isn't the dark ages. What are you afraid of? The legality? The morality?"

I shook my head again. I knew this child inside me, felt I had known her before I was born, and I knew I was keeping her. I just wasn't going to talk about it, except to say, "I'm going to name this kid 'Spontaneity.'"

"That's not very funny," Jack said glumly.

* * *

There followed two weeks of thick, troubled impasse. It boiled over in Jack late one night as I came through the door, carrying my shoes in my hand.

"All right," he insisted, seemingly taking up some angry conversation he'd already been having with me in his mind. "I've decided. Having a baby is out of the question."

I wasn't about to listen to an ultimatum. I threw my own back at him. "No, Jack. What's out of the question is an abortion."

He glared at me, eyebrows crushed together in indictment of my willfulness. "You always think you can have it whatever way you want. Well, this time you will have to choose. Do you want a husband or do you want a baby?"

I laughed. "You mean, which baby do I want? The husband or the one in here?" I patted my belly.

Jack sputtered.

"There is no choice! Jack, this is too easy. This baby is mine. It's the only thing in this life that belongs to me. If you want to move out, move out. It won't bother me a bit. I don't need two babies!"

I looked then at Jack. That vein over his temple was throbbing ominously, looking like a swollen river. I realized that although he hadn't made any gestures, any threats to me, that I was stooped in a cowering position. My words masked my fear.

The shock of my own vulnerability swarmed over me with a wave of panic, and I felt almost physically sick. I was no longer responsible only for myself, my seemingly indestructible self, never ill and unable to feel pain. Now I was two. Now there was another inside me, her safety was my charge, and her health depended on mine. My long-running feelings of detachment were a thing of the past, at least as far as this other life in my womb was concerned.

Jack went to Lucien's without even taking his slippers.

* * *

I asked for more hours at the restaurant. I would need every cent I could make now. I had three good friends at work, all Puerto Rican, and one night we all went to Spanish Harlem to dance. I insisted on taking the bus home, not wanting to spend money for cab fare. Angelo, a Brass Rail busboy, waited with me in the rain and rode downtown with me.

He saw me to my door and I asked him to come in. I knew that he'd heard about my husband's book, and that he admired writers and poets. But Angelo's upbringing had been strict in regard to moral conduct, especially where married women are concerned, and he was reluctant to come inside. I assured him that he was welcome in my home, that Jack was gone, and that it would be my pleasure to make him a cup of coffee and show him the copy of

The Town and the City that Jack had given me the first day we met.

We debated in the rain. Finally Angelo decided the coffee was too tempting, and he would come in for a moment. I put the pot on and showed him Jack's picture on the cover of *The Town and the City*. Angelo spoke no English. I opened the book and read from the first page, translating the text for him.

Suddenly, we heard knuckles rapping at the door. Angelo ran, intuitively, to the window. It was stuck, and while I shouted to him that there was no need to worry, Jack yelled from outside, "What's going on in there?"

Jack used his key to unlock the door, and he hurled it open. The minute the door budged, Angelo dashed out under Jack's arm. Jack jumped back, then, "What was that all about?" he asked furiously.

I told Jack where we'd been, how I had asked Angelo in, and why he was afraid. It was obvious from the order of the room that nothing amiss had transpired. There wasn't so much as a wrinkle in the bedspread. But Jack's eyes had lit up by this point.

"How do I know you haven't been running around with that spic for the past two months?"

"How about, because I only met him two weeks ago."

"Or some other spic! How do I know what you do with your time when I'm out?"

I wanted to lean into his face and unleash the most unearthly scream I could muster, but instead I ground my teeth together and seethed. "Did you come over to get your stuff?" I asked in a white fury. "Then get it! And take your paranoia and type it onto a toilet paper roll and flush it down the toilet!"

* * *

I had given up. It was over, and I began to make plans to move back to my mother's house in Albany County. I felt a deep sense of failure, underneath the turmoil of every other emotion. I had failed to make any real human connection, of love or friendship or caring of any type. Jack hated me, and I felt completely indifferent. My love with Herb had ended in simple escape, but this unhappy marriage of mine would end in bitterness and enmity. And more and more, now, I began to think of Bill. I wished for his advice, the words of my big brother all. I mourned him in a way I had not at the time of his death; by feeling a deep sense of loss that he wasn't with me.

When Jack called and said that he wanted to talk one more time, and asked me to meet him on the rooftop of Lucien's building, I was stung with an anguished sense that he knew how much I missed Bill, and that he wanted to burn me with it until I cried out for mercy. The mere mention of the place embroiled me in memories of Bill, of chasing him across rooftops wrapped in sheets, of the way he would sometimes gaze across the buildings of his city.

But I wasn't willing for Jack to know how much it hurt, and I agreed to meet him there.

Standing in the warm night, waiting for him to arrive, I looked across the lights of New York and lost myself in a reverie. *Grandfather*, I murmured in my mind. *I had a beautiful, perfect web, and now it has been destroyed by the sunlight.*

Finally, Jack arrived. I had assumed we were going to talk about a divorce. But Jack had another question on his mind.

"What if I said you could have the baby? What then?"

I looked at him in the still night air for a long time, wondering. Is he giving me another chance at a bad marriage? Asking for another chance for himself? Or is the question purely hypothetical?

"I don't need your permission," I told him finally. "Or want it, either."

He turned on his heel and stalked downstairs. After a while I started down too. Passing by Lucien's door, I heard Jack shouting, "All right! I asked her! And she won't have me back! Now don't tell me that kid's my responsibility. I don't ever want to hear about it again."

And now I whispered to myself again as I hurried down the hall, this time to the big brother I'd found and then lost. *Bill,* I silently prayed. *Why did you ever bring us together? Why did you ever think it could work?*

Why did you leave me, Bill?

Chapter Twenty

This would be the end of my glamorous independent life in the city—it was over. I couldn't stay in Manhattan any longer. I felt heartsick, now, every time I thought of Bill, Jack, Herb, all the friends that would now side with Jack, and even my own friend Sarah. And beyond that desperate unhappiness, the practical truth was that I couldn't afford to stay.

I called my mother and, with a crushed spirit, made arrangements with her to return by train to Albany. I gave notice at the restaurant, told the landlord I had to give up the apartment, and began to pack the few belongings that meant anything to me.

On the morning of my last day in New York City, bags latched and waiting by the door, sitting nervously with two hours to go before it would be time to leave for Penn Station, I picked up the phone and made the call I dreaded but knew I must make. I dialed Paul Blake's number, and when Caroline picked up the phone, I asked to speak to Gabe.

What I had in mind was to soften the blow of the breakup, to try to make sure Gabe didn't hate me, to assure her that I'd keep in touch and that she'd see her grandchild. But Jack had already called her, as it turned out, and the conversation didn't go the way I expected, not at all.

"Oh, Ti-Jeanne," Gabe wailed into the phone. "I am very sad, because you are a good girl."

"Thank you, Gabe. I will miss you very much. And—"

"But thanks to God," Gabe interrupted, "thanks to God you are not pregnant."

I stopped short, my mouth open. "But. . ." I stammered. "But I. . ."

There was a long silence in the conversation while I tried to work this out. Why would Jack have told her I was not pregnant? Then the freight train of an answer roared through my head. Gabe would have insisted we get back together. She would never have allowed Jack to leave his child.

For a brief instant I was angry at Jack, and in the next moment I was even more angry at myself. I would have blithely told her about the baby, and then she would have bent heaven and earth to keep us together. I wanted that even less than Jack did. So now I must hold my tongue. I drew in my breath.

"Ti-Jeanne?"

"Yes, Gabe, I'm here."

"What did Jackie do? Did he hurt you, Ti-Jeanne? If he hurt you. . ."

"No... no." I hesitated again, trying to know what to say to her. "It was nobody's fault, Gabe," I finally told her. "It just didn't work out. I guess I didn't love him. You were right, Gabe, you knew. I didn't love him. We are both sorry, but it just didn't work out."

I could hear Gabe nodding. Finally she said, "Go with God, Ti-Jeanne."

"*Adieu,* Gabe."

I placed the phone slowly in the cradle and held my hand on it and stood by the window. As if I were holding my fingers over a wood stove on a snowy night, warmth began to roll slowly through me. With it came a dawning sense that my life and my soul were finally beginning to return to me. I'd missed them so intensely. Finally, I could be free. Free of this marriage and its obligations, free because I had come out of it on my own terms, without strings.

I was returning to my mother's house. But now I was about to be a mother myself. I'd lived on my own, had a marriage, and kissed it goodbye to bring a new person into the world.

I was bound to this tiny life inside me. But she was my choice, my dream. I wanted her more than anything. A feeling of exhilaration raced through me now, and I stood up and smiled and stretched my hands into the air in pure happiness. She was mine, my child. She'd have Kerouac blood, she might even have the Kerouac face and features. And maybe she'd even possess a Kerouac literary gift. But she'd grow up with me, learn to see the world through me. In homage to my grandfather, I'd be with her as she learned to spin her own dew-sparkled webs. And if I raised her to think for herself and to value learning and to ask questions and be honest, maybe she'd take the Kerouac legacy one step further:

Maybe she would write the truth.

1978

It was the week after Thanksgiving, dark by five o'clock now, and cold in eastern Washington. Walking home from work, I approached my house, the tall red one on North Ruby Street. Glancing up at the windows of our apartment, I wondered if Jan and David, my oldest and youngest, were at home, and if anything had been started for dinner. In case it hadn't, I pulled my coat tightly against the wind gusting down the street and continued another block up the hill to the supermarket. I'd get something quick for dinner, saving time for the letter I must compose soliciting questions for a survey to be taken as part of a VISTA project. My partner on the project and I had recently returned from a week's training. She, more pessimistic than I, had doubts about our being able to complete our task in the allotted time. I, however, refused to see the obstacles. After a ten year, self-imposed exile (or was it some kind of penance?) in a cabin several miles out of town, I had moved into Ellensburg for just such a job opportunity, seeing in it only what I wished to see.

And there was also the university, only a stone's throw from my house, beckoning to me with a myriad of courses in philosophy and sociology and genetics and who knew what other delights. For the first time in thirty years I had a plan for my life, some particular goals to achieve. I felt competent, confident, even efficient, equal to the challenges of continuing my education in middle age.

As I entered the kitchen of our apartment, carrying a bag of groceries, the phone rang in the living room. "David...Jan...

Could one of you get that..? I heard the muffled sounds of David's voice answering the call.

"Mom, it's for you. The guy who called earlier."

"What guy?" I asked, as I set the groceries on the kitchen counter and headed toward the living room. David capped the receiver with his hand.

"Dunno. Wouldn't say."

He gave me the phone. I glanced at him leaving the room as I held the receiver up to my ear. "Hello..."

The answering voice was low and soft and familiar. It swirled about me like a tide of warm water as it carried me back over the years, to a few times like this when it had taken me by surprise, and to nearly thirty years ago when it had spoken to me in the closeness of a lovemaking embrace. My breath caught, knees went weak. My God, I was just a young girl again. The few times I'd been in touch with him over the decades my reaction was always the same. Old wounds were in danger of being opened and I was on the alert—but essentially helpless.

"Herb!"

"You recognized my voice. That's amazing."

"Where are you?"

Right here. Still in Maryland."

"The same address? 1500 Pooks Hill Road?"

"How did you remember that?"

Chitchat. That gave me a little strength, or at least the illusion of it. "I never forget anything. How did you find me? I don't even have the same name."

"I did some detective work. Started with City Lights in San Francisco after Jan had an excerpt from her book published in their journal. Guess she's in New York now."

"She's here. Arrived just before Thanksgiving."

Jan and David came into the room, curious to know who I was talking to. "It's an old friend," I told them.

"Tell them I'm *very* old. Fifty-six and a half." Smiling, I repeated it to my kids.

"So, how does it feel to have been close to greatness?" Herb asked.

"Greatness?"

"The interest in your first husband seems to be reviving. All kinds of books about him. And movies. Do you know Carolyn Cassady?"

"No."

"She wrote a book abou—"

"I know."

"Did you read it?"

"Yes. Standing up in a store. I'd be damned if I was going to buy it."

"*You* should write a book, Joan. You were married to him."

"I am writing one."

"Wonderful!"

"But mine isn't just about Jack. I can't write that story without including you and Bill Cannastra."

"*I'm* in your book?"

"Sure. Weren't you there when I met Jack?" Having settled into some degree of ease, I ventured to voice what I most wanted to know. "Why did you call, Herb? To urge me to write a book?"

"...No. Because of the past...and because I was...afraid that something might happen to you."

"What could happen that hasn't already?"

"Guess I just wanted to be satisfied that you were alright. I have a friend whose son recently died in a fishing accident. It brought up my fears. You never know when something like that is going to happen."

"I know. I've been apprehensive about your health and safety for years...The last time I heard from you was that card with the Indian basket weaver on it. I felt you were putting me down so I didn't write back."

"What did it say on it?"

"Wasn't what you said. It was the caption: 'Anything I can't stand, it's a smart alecky basket weaver.'"

He laughed. "Haven't you learned not to take me seriously?"

"I've tried." There was a mutual pause that Herb relieved.

"How are your other kids? The twins?"

"Kathy's fine. She was here for Thanksgiving dinner. But I haven't seen Sharon for a couple of years. They live in Eugene, Oregon...Are you in touch with your daughter Karen?"

"Of course. We spend a great deal of time together. She has a place in the Village now. I showed her where you and I used to live before they tore down the building."

"...Oh, it's gone?" Feeling sad, I was taken aback by his flippant response.

"Yup. Sacrificed to urban renewal...Joan, I really think we should see each other. Will you be free Christmastime?"

Evasively, I told him how limited my time was then, what with my involvement with VISTA and all, and we talked about the possibility of our getting together the following spring or summer.

After we hung up, I realized, as I'm sure Herb did also, that by not making firm plans we each had preserved some magic. Our bond was unbroken after all these years, but unfinished business was what sustained us. In momentary fantasy I imagined that maybe we could reap the reward of so many years apart if we dug up the past and examined it carefully, finally resolving our issues.

But reality soon became obvious. We didn't see the same things as issues. Our priorities were different and, as before, we didn't think alike, speak the same language. We were fated to an attraction so beset by short circuiting it couldn't last in any constant way. Our unresolved relationship was always there, not at the forefront at all times, but nagging in the background of everything I did, probably everything he did, exemplifying all the failures and misconceptions in each of our lives. Our obligations unfulfilled, dreams unrealized.

If we could have found that elusive way of being, a graceful blend of give and take, we might've had the basic understanding of all that was important to us, together and separately. But each of us had our unrelenting self-assertion. If Herb and I were meant to be together in some lifetime or other it wasn't this one. The most we were capable of now was just wishing the other well.

But had I ever really expected more than that?